Praise for *Bad Mormon*

"A spicy debut ... by turns cheeky and reflective ... *Real Housewives* disciples will relish these unfiltered revelations."

—*Publishers Weekly*

"A thoughtful, smart, and funny handbook for apostates."

—*Kirkus Reviews*

"Frank, funny, and irreverent, *Bad Mormon* captures the spirit of the woman millions have come to love/hate on TV. Even those unfamiliar with the show will be fascinated by her detailed descriptions ... *The Real Housewives of Salt Lake City* is a TV sensation, and Gay is the breakout star, so expect a lot of interest in her story of her religious journey."

—*Booklist*

"Gay's book is raw and revealing, an eye-opening firsthand account of religious indoctrination told with candor and sincerity."

—*Interview Magazine*

"Gay's book has major stakes: In tracing her journey from aspiring housewife to capital-H Housewife, she writes about Mormonism's sacred rituals in a manner that is not only grounds for excommunication in the church but also risks ostracization from the entire community she held dear for so long."

—*Bustle*

"[A] confident debut."

—*The Daily Beast*

"No stone goes unturned."

—*PEOPLE*

"[Gay's] charismatic personality shines on the show. That same charm is also abundantly evident in her memoir . . . Recommended for fans of the show, of course. This memoir will also appeal to [those] who enjoy reading about women successfully navigating adulthood and motherhood."

—*Library Journal*

"Gay's story and internal battle will likely resonate with anybody who grew up having a complicated relationship with organized religion."

—*The Cut*

"Heather Gay's *Bad Mormon* pulls back the curtain on LDS—and— Real Housewife-hood."

—*New York Magazine*, Approval Matrix

"The book offers a drastic juxtaposition between the Heather Gay that once was and the Heather Gay of today."

—Today.com

GOOD TIME GIRL

ALSO BY HEATHER GAY

Bad Mormon

GOOD TIME GIRL

HEATHER GAY

GALLERY BOOKS
New York   London   Toronto   Sydney   New Delhi

G

Gallery Books
An Imprint of Simon & Schuster, LLC
1230 Avenue of the Americas
New York, NY 10020

First Gallery Books hardcover edition December 2024

GALLERY BOOKS and colophon are registered trademarks of Simon & Schuster, LLC

Simon & Schuster: Celebrating 100 Years of Publishing in 2024

For information about special discounts for bulk purchases, please contact Simon & Schuster Special Sales at 1-866-506-1949 or business@simonandschuster.com.

The Simon & Schuster Speakers Bureau can bring authors to your live event. For more information or to book an event, contact the Simon & Schuster Speakers Bureau at 1-866-248-3049 or visit our website at www.simonspeakers.com.

Interior design by Jaime Putorti

Manufactured in the United States of America

10 9 8 7 6 5 4 3 2 1

Library of Congress Cataloging-in-Publication Data is available upon request.

ISBN 978-1-6680-4980-8
ISBN 978-1-6680-4982-2 (ebook)

This book is a memoir. It reflects my present recollections of experiences over time. Some names and characteristics have been changed, some events have been compressed, and some dialogue has been reconstructed.

To Members of the Pink Pony Club Everywhere,

Keep on Dancing!

CONTENTS

CONTENTS

INTRODUCTION

In 1997, an entrepreneur with serious frat-boy energy started an adult entertainment company that would later become a cultural sensation. He created films that invited the audience into the raunchy, no-rules, no-regrets world of college-aged kids celebrating Spring Break. Camera crews and producers infiltrated boozy party locations and filmed girls getting naked and getting frisky in exchange for merchandise advertising the film's title and juggernaut brand.

These films didn't feature girls that went through the theater program at Yale to become professional actresses. These films didn't feature girls that went on to walk the runway for New York Fashion Week as professional models. These films didn't even feature girls that worked their way up through the ranks of the adult-film industry. The stars of these films were the mostly ordinary (some extraordinary) girls you'd see walking every day on campus. They were the girls next door, the girls you went to class with, the girls just like you and me. They were the Girls Gone Wild.

The public could not get enough, and the *Girls Gone Wild* brand exploded practically overnight, creating over three hundred films, a clothing line, a recorded album, and even a magazine. Within five years, that frat-boy entrepreneur, Joe Francis, sold over 4.5 million copies of *Girls Gone Wild*, elevating the brazen antics of college girls everywhere into a profitable phenomenon. Production value was low; titillation value was high. And for the next decade, these videos defined the debauchery found on college campuses across America. *Girls Gone Wild* became the female version of John Belushi's *Animal House*.

I was a college-aged girl during the height of this era, but perhaps not surprisingly, Joe Francis's cameras never made it over to my campus at Brigham Young University in Provo, Utah—also known as Happy Valley. I never took a Spring Break trip, nor entered a wet T-shirt contest. The closest I got to baring my breasts was going topless in a tanning bed in my tiny landlocked corner of the world. I wasn't going anywhere, but if anyone had asked, this girl would've gone wild.

But somehow, during season 1 of *The Real Housewives of Salt Lake City*, through a series of misremembered events, I became branded as a tit-flashing, Honor Code–denying girl who *had* gone wild. In a true Housewife mix-up, I was called a Good-Time Girl. The name stung not only because it was untrue, but also because it reminded me of a life unlived.

For most of my life, I was taught only to be good: to be a good girl in a bad world, happy with anything, satisfied with less than her share. But I learned very quickly that good girls were usually small and meek. They were valued not for their independence and ingenuity, but for their submission and sweetness. Good girls didn't seek bigger lives; they didn't long to be immortalized like the Girls Gone Wild, even if just in late-night infomercials for direct-to-DVD videos. They shunned the spotlight and suffered in silence. They didn't long to expand their cultural horizons—to travel, to eat, to drink, to love. And, perhaps above all, good girls never craved a good time.

I sacrificed a lot to obtain the brass rings of a good Mormon life: I was abstinent till marriage, I served an eighteen-month mission, and I married in the temple. But try as I might to stay small and grateful, I never quite felt fulfilled. There was always a part of me that felt incomplete, maybe even dishonest. And it wasn't until I lost everything—my marriage, my family, my church, my community—that I recognized what that part was, the truest part of myself that I'd buried and ignored in order to fit in. Who I am at my core contradicted the person my family and church wanted me to be. Because at the end of the day, while I may have said I wanted a small, good life, if I was really honest, all I ever wanted was a big, extraordinary one.

I've always had a voracious appetite for new experiences, and I've sought to expand my worldview at every turn. I've worked tirelessly to find any crack in the veneer of perfection so as to let the hot lava of life flow through. Whether imagining dime-sized frogs in San Bernardino to be the sounds of the Amazon rainforest, or kissing a burly bar hand in Tijuana on my high school senior trip, I've always been a true romantic and have viewed my life through rose-colored lenses, waiting anxiously to partake in all of its untold wonder. I've always wanted to grab the world with both hands and never let it go, but I felt ashamed and guilty for wanting those things.

Being on television has given me privilege and access like I've never had before, but more than that it's given me permission to embrace myself fully, to embrace the exhilaration of living out your wildest dreams and not apologizing for it. I'm still the same person I've always been, but now the doors have been opened to live the life I dreamed of. I've finally returned to the girl who wasn't afraid to be unabashedly herself, the adventurer looking around every corner for an experience more exciting, enriching, and enlightening than the last. If I've learned anything over the course of my life, it's that you can't outrun yourself. Wherever you go, there you are.

When it came time to think of titles for this book, *Good Time Girl* surfaced to the top of the list right away. I'm reclaiming the title as a positive attribute rather than the character flaw it was originally used as. And I'm embracing the nickname not for all that it promised to be, but for all that it's proven to become.

There is no amount of hiding or fronting that can truly change who you are meant to be. It doesn't matter if you're good, bad, or Mormon; at the end of the day, I just want to live my life as authentically as possible while mustering up as much friendship and laughter as I can. And for now, I'm just trying to find the honor in that.

I'm getting a second chance to experience the unlived life I longed for. I am finally honoring not the wildness of the world, but the wildness within me, and I'm not afraid to embrace it . . . Honor Code, what?!

ONE

GOOD-TIME GIRL

I would've loved to have been a Good-Time Girl in college!" Really, I would've loved to have been *anything* in college. I would've loved to have experienced day drinking, a hangover, a one-night stand. The truth is, I was not a Good-Time Girl. And worse, I wasn't even adjacent to any Good-Time Girls. In fact, no one I knew in college was having a good time at all by any standard definition. We were at a no-sex, no-drinking, no-fraternizing church-owned university, where good times were relegated to Star Wars theme parties and Family Home Evening groups.

I knew what college was supposed to be like; I had seen the movies and had visited Greek Row at the University of Utah. But Brigham Young University (BYU) was not like any college ever represented on-screen or off. Everything was loaded, fraught with potential judgment: who you dated, what you studied, how you worked, how you relaxed. We were observing each other, noting everyone's level of righteousness, devotion to the faith, and ability to be a good husband or wife in the future. I can't remember going to one single college party in the traditional sense. No red Solo cups, no socks on the door handles, no keg stands. I can't remember even hearing about a house party, and if there was one, I'm sure it was no wilder than a game of Twister, fully clothed, with a couple of empty two-liter bottles of Sprite. Twister and Sprite is not necessarily a *Bad* Time, but it's definitely not the image that popped to mind the first time I heard the phrase "Good-Time Girl." That image was one of a college co-ed on Spring Break in microshorts with a tank top yanked up to her chin. A Mardi Gras girl flashing all her fellow students. But there were neither beads nor Bourbon Street at BYU. If I flashed anyone, it could have only been by accident. An inadvertent act done during a heated game of Twister while trying to place my right hand onto someone else's blue circle.

There were no sororities, no fraternities, no wet T-shirt contests. No actual twisting of body parts off the Hasbro mat. Like the aliens sang about life on Mars in the movie *Waiting for Guffman*, "BORING! BORING! BORING!" These were quintessential college experiences I wanted to have, but I didn't know where to find them, or where to even find the BYU version of them. If you don't drink in college, what do you even really do? If a Good-Time Girl flashes her tits in the forest, does it even make a sound if she's completely sober? Imagine how brazen you'd have to be to live a Mardi Gras life on a tap water cocktail . . .

Yet, somehow, despite all of these factors, the nickname was bestowed upon me years after it was impossible to prove otherwise. It came about through a story that is pretty embarrassing. It all began when I was twelve years old, sowing my wild oats at a Brigham Young University summer retreat called Academy for Girls. It was the closest thing to a military academy that my parents could find that didn't involve shaving my head or wearing a uniform.

Academy for Girls was specifically designed for girls in the Church of Jesus Christ of Latter-Day Saints between the ages of twelve and eighteen from all over the world. We came to Provo, Utah, to experience the BYU campus for six spiritually uplifting, platitude-packed days and five fun-filled nights. We stayed in the freshman dorms and attended classes on etiquette, poise, handicrafts, religion, and homemaking. There were no boys and no Mardi Gras beads, but there were definitely boobs—two on every attendee, in fact. We heard mention of one coed activity, a dance held with the neighboring Academy for Boys, but that was only for the girls who were fourteen and up. I, at a pudgy, prepubescent twelve, wasn't eligible for that type of fun, so I had to create my own.

Our counselor stayed on the same floor as us in a locked room at the end of the hallway. Once she went to bed, it was hard to rouse her, and it was after lights-out that we had our best adventures. Each counselor went by a made-up name she chose for herself in order to give an air of anonymity and an extra element of fun. My counselor chose the nickname Kare, spelled K-A-R-E, as in Care Bear with a funky K—which I thought was a fail and a less than valiant effort. When I learned later that Kare was just short for her real name, Karrie, I knew my instincts had been right. She was phoning it in! It felt like a rip-off, especially when I met the other camp counselors who had names like Lickety Splits and Rainbow Sunshine. Meanwhile, I got stuck with Kare . . . spelled wrong. Like many things in my twelve-year-old girl's life, it was a letdown.

Our days were spent dressed in modest attire, attending seminars in giant auditoriums on campus. We ate in the cafeteria, and every other day we had supervised outings. Our excursions were held on campus and limited to Navajo tacos in the Cougareat and visits to the BYU Creamery for a single scoop of ice cream—vanilla, mostly.

Part of our requirement at Academy for Girls was memorizing the standards that were listed explicitly in the official church pamphlet, *For the Strength of Youth*. It was a two-by-three paper notebook outlining a clear set of criteria that all devout Mormon kids should aspire to. It dictated appropriate hairstyles, appropriate clothing choices, and appropriate physical adornments. In the fine print, it made crystal clear that there should be no more than one piercing per earlobe.

Naively, I thought the only place you could get a piercing was an earlobe and that it only happened at Claire's boutique in your local shopping mall. It involved a highly trained, but definitely not OSHA-certified store clerk, and what may or may not have been a medical-device piercing gun. But, as I learned this fateful night, if you have a needle, an ice cube, and a willing accomplice, you can pierce just about anything just about anywhere . . . and Academy for Girls, seemed as good a place as any.

I didn't know I wanted a second piercing until they told me I couldn't have one. This was my only chance. I had barely gotten my parents to take me to Claire's for my initial piercing, and there was no way I could convince them to take me for a second round.

I volunteered to go first. I wanted to establish myself as the bravest, most rebellious one in the group. We set up our makeshift clinic in the room farthest from our counselors with added pillows squeezed into the space between the carpet and the door frame to muffle the sound of my screams. Four girls held me down while my friend Aimee numbed my earlobe with a melting ice cube—I can still feel the trickle of water that trailed down my neck and into the collar of my shirt. She took a needle and sprayed it with hair spray because "the alcohol will kill the germs" and proceeded to slowly, with zero finesse, push the needle through the lobe of my ear. Every single layer of flesh give way with an audible pop. I barely survived the first earlobe without passing out before I managed to tell the group through sweaty tears that I needed a break. I took a few melty ice cubes and my bruised ego back to my room. As I left, I promised we could pierce the other earlobe the following night, but we all knew it was a lie. Regret had set in like a thick blanket over the thrill of rebellion, and I took the rogue earring out the next morning hoping that the hole would seal before my parents arrived for the final banquet.

Disappointed in my cowardice, I now had something to prove.

The next day, by luck or divine providence, we discovered an old wheelchair in a utility closet on our dorm room floor. One of the girls in our group got in the chair and pulled a twin-sized blanket over her head as if she were some sort of crazed patient from a mental facility. Taking my cue, I joined in, playing the role of Unhinged Nurse. I embraced my reign of terror and seized the opportunity to rebel anew. Once the lights were out, we began barging into girls' rooms unannounced. My crazed patient would fling open the door to a room, and I would push the wheelchair as fast as I could straight up to the victim's bedside and scream, "BOOBIES!" Then, from under the blanket, she would reach out and attempt to give the girl a titty twister. It was pretty hard for her to find the titties given the blanket, the darkness of the room, and the girl's terrified screams. I did my best to guide and direct her outstretched hands with slight adjustments to the wheelchair. From

behind, I pushed and pivoted and encouraged her to "Grab higher!"
and "To the right! To the right! You're skimming her elbow!" We only
retreated when contact was actually made. Every tit must be twisted!
The wheelchair moved sluggishly across the Berber-carpeted floors,
but I was amped up on adrenaline and my new persona and found
the strength to invade as many rooms as possible before our counselor,
Kare, woke up and shut down our reign of terror.

As I had secretly hoped and prayed, this little prank reestablished
me as a rule breaker. The Terrorizing Titty-Twister Twins were talked
about far and wide. As notorious as I felt then, I was equally as confident that once I walked off campus, that reputation and its sins would
be far behind me. But I should have known that God never forgets. I
never repented appropriately, and because I hadn't taken it to Him in
prayer, He in turn sent it right back down into the hands of Lisa Barlow. Which, even next to the legendary wrath of God, was much more
damning.

Flash forward three decades to 2019 and the reveal of the cast
of *The Real Housewives of Salt Lake City*. After hearing our names
announced together for the first season, Lisa Barlow discovered that
her neighbor also knew me. We hadn't seen each other since we were
teens at the Academy for Girls, but apparently, I had left an impression. My reputation as the nefarious Titty Twister had followed me.
It was the one anecdote she remembered, and she readily shared it
with Lisa, who proceeded to conflate a lot of the details. And sure,
Lisa might not be the greatest listener, but considering the facts, even
I would have been confused: "I knew Heather . . . BYU . . . a lot of
fun . . . boobies! . . . Got in trouble . . . pretty wild." Based on those

CliffsNotes, Lisa assumed that this was a tale about college coeds in their early twenties.

This was a side to me that Lisa had never imagined. And yet . . . it tracked. Suddenly, I was a Good-Time Girl: "Heather Gay thinks every day is Mardi Gras at BYU"; "Honor Code, what?!" Boobs and blankets at twelve somehow turned into flashing and flirting at twenty.

Perhaps that's why, when I first heard about the accusation in season 1 of *Salt Lake City*, I found it so offensive. I had never even been to Mardi Gras, let alone earned a string of beads. But I had seen *The Real World: New Orleans* and the fun that they had, and it rubbed me the wrong way. As a student, I worked forty hours a week at two jobs, took a full course load, started a small business, and did everything I could to scrape by. And yet here I was, wearing the scarlet letter without having had any of the scarlet fun. *I would've loved to have been a Good-Time Girl in college!*

Once I didn't have to hide, I realized that Lisa Barlow had it right all along (Of course she did!). I was born a Good-Time Girl, and now I'm less afraid to say it out loud. It's easily the truest, wildest, most authentic part of myself. But for most of my life, it was also the part of myself that I thought was weak, rebellious, and wrong. The life that had been ascribed to me did not make room for Good-Time Girls, only Good Little Girls, and that ideology was reinforced in every interaction I had with my parents, my siblings, my teachers, my friends, and my church. I tried to hide who I was like the world's worst-kept secret.

Following season 1, when I started to work on the first draft of my memoir, *Bad Mormon*, I began going through all my old scrapbooks and journals and stumbled upon letters reminding me that this had never really been a secret. One letter in particular was written to my best friend when I was twenty-three, just a few weeks before I finished my missionary service in the South of France. During this eighteen-month-long mission, my life had been dedicated to daily prayer, scripture study, and full-time service. My every waking moment was entrenched in serving the Lord and proclaiming the Gospel. Every thought, every conversation, every agenda was about God, getting closer to God, bringing people to God, and becoming more like God. I talked to thousands of people, bearing my testimony daily in French and in English, about His eternal Plan of Happiness and my hopeful eternal glory.

And even after ALL of that, I still couldn't purge myself of the desire to want more. In the letter, I confided my fears and my dreams—the tangible longing for a bigger life, the acknowledgment of the real me screaming to get out. It's who I always was, and I knew it even back then. I tried to fill my bucket with enough illicit reserves to get me through the life that was planned for me, but it wasn't enough. It was never enough. To get more, I'd have to give up the safety and control that I'd been taught to aspire to. And now I'm beginning to believe that my ambition isn't something to be ashamed of; it might even be my greatest attribute.

Now I have the perspective of someone who has made bad choices and still been "blessed." The Mormon part of me still clings to the belief that my current success and happiness are not real. That any temporary blessings are fruit from the Poison Tree and can never last. But I'm trying to remember that this is a lie. In fact, it's the exact opposite. I didn't get here because I betrayed my church or my family; I got here because I stopped betraying myself.

Now, with perspective, the nickname of Good-Time Girl is something I'm proud to claim. After all, it's much cooler than Kare with a funky K. I'll wear my scarlet "GTG" proudly emblazoned on my chest, and I'll be delighted that she finally feels welcome.

TWO

I DON'T WANT TO BE
"VERY HAPPY"

Below is a letter written to my best friend in April 1998, in response
to a letter and cassette tape that she sent me while I was a missionary
serving in the South of France. Out of respect for the person I was
then and the person I've never been able to outrun, the words have
been transcribed exactly as they were originally written.

Dear Marjorie —

*It is a rainy day here on the Côte d'Azur. I'm sitting here listen-
ing to your tape for the second time. I can't say thank you enough.*

*I'm aching — ACHING — listening to your voice, listening
to the bootleg music, and listening to the voices of our friends. I'm
instinctively responding like we are in a live conversation, offering
random comments, laughter, and direct counsel with intuitive sen-
sitivity. It is frightening to hear the voices of high school friends and
realize 1) Nothing has really changed, 2) All these wonderful people*

are in Utah and I'm going to Colorado, and 3) I am just as geeky as they all seem to be. Reality check: now I'm actually even GEEKIER!

Here's a humbling statement: I'm going to be an R.M. [Return Missionary] (Gag!). Does this mean no more frenzied blackjack sprees in backless shirts at your condo in Vegas? Does this mean I am automatically labeled as a) Horny (crude, I know), b) Desperate, and c) Husband hunting? All three of which are terms I have unfortunately frequently heard employed and am absolutely disgusted by. Help me! Help me!

I just twirled and danced to the bootleg Shawn Colvin, Linda Ronstadt, James Taylor, etc. medley you recorded for me with utter ease. It is a total thunderstorm here. I'm sitting on the terrace of our fifth-story apartment building, cherishing the sensation. The lightning flashes, the surging traffic flows (water on wheels almost sounds like a river at night . . . or maybe not). I'm absorbing every moment of this blissful solitude. In French, they say "il pleut des cordes," which means quite literally, "it's raining ropes." Now I understand the source of this expression. It is as if white ropes of water are streaming from the sky. I want to call you, but it's three o'clock in the morning your time, and I doubt you'd be up for some chitchat.

Back to the subject: I'm ready for reality. I ACHE for reality: namely Men, Music, and Movies. The three big M's, baby.

I got my hair cut yesterday at the salon. Pascal, a blue-eyed, goateed, twenty-five-year-old Parisian, was my stylist. He flirted with me so outrageously, I was blushing. Me blushing! He totally didn't grasp the concept of missionary. I was like, "Pascal, I am like a NUN. Could I be more clear?" He nevertheless secretly handed me his card and whispered in my ear to hide it and to give him a call. Can you say temptation?

My new companion is awake. Her name is Mary Pierce from Centerville, Utah. She met her "future husband" in her last area. They've exchanged CTR [Choose The Right] rings and are "getting married" April 18. Next year, obviously, because they want to honorably finish their missions. It's all she's talked about since she's arrived . . . how she's his first love. He's twenty, and she's had this spiritual confirmation [about their relationship], and now it's just a matter of time. GAG ME! Seriously, how can people think that way? I'm not kidding. It's as if getting married is asking someone to "go with you" in fifth grade. The grossest part is [that] I have to sit there and talk to her and be sensitive and listen when what I really want to do is hurl. It'll be a fun four weeks with her. I'll do my best to help her realize that it's important to see your future husband in other circumstances than an isolated city in the South of France as a missionary. It's stories like this that make me think I'll never get married because I could never in 1 million years fall in love with someone like that.

I'm ready to come home. In a lot of ways, I think that my spiritual awareness and testimony will actually grow and strengthen as a direct result of being home. I don't feel like I'm in a spiritual bubble as a missionary, but more like an open wound that keeps taking hits. I look forward to the cocoon of fellow saints and eternal family, gospel topics other than baptism and church attendance. I'm glad I won't have to explain away polygamy, racism, and the fact that I am unable to watch TV, listen to music, or visit Paris during my stay in France.

Mediocrity is a great void that frightens me to my very core, but I feel myself pulled toward it daily. It's a constant struggle. It's something I never discuss with anyone, but the truth is, I don't want to be normal. I don't want to get married, have children, and be "very happy." I want to be a superstar. I want to live an extraordinary life. I want to be Kate Winslet or Toni Morrison or Ann Landers or Barbara Walters etc. Don't mock me. I don't know what I need to do, but I know it's something. And I am so afraid of not accomplishing it. Plus, there's this whole other part of me that says I'm too full of pride, I seek the glory of the world, the glory of men, and that my "ambitions" are contrary to the laws of God and the laws of the Gospel. My divine role is not to change the world, but to build a family. I know all this, and I can't accept that I'm still wrestling with the ever present battle of carnal versus spiritual that has haunted me all my life, as it does everyone I guess. It's an issue I can't really express in this letter.

Marjorie, I love you. You are a powerful, amazing woman. Just know that you are an inspiration and an example to me of duty and righteousness. I trust you with my soul. Keep the faith. I'll see you very soon.

Love —

Heath

THREE

SAN BERNARDINO

I 've always been a dreamer, from the rainy balcony on the Cote d' Azur to the window perch of my childhood home. As a little girl, I'd look out onto our picturesque cul-de-sac on a quiet street in suburban Denver, Colorado, and dream of a world that existed beyond my horizon.

I was a voracious reader, and I had a wildly active imagination, diving into every book I read like it was happening to me in real life. *Mrs. Piggle Wiggle* books were my favorite, a series of children's books that could've been the inspiration for the TV show *Supernanny*. I loved the tales of incorrigible children, their exasperated parents, and the magic and creativity of Mrs. Piggle Wiggle, who would swoop in to solve their behavioral problems with wit and charm. I rooted for the naughty kids and secretly hoped at least one of them would be able to withstand the logic and tactics of Mrs. Piggle Wiggle. But I also empathized with the frustrated parents and the horrors of having an errant child. If anything, I identified the most with, of course the main character, the supernanny,

Mrs. Piggle Wiggle herself. A loving and wise friend to all, a woman that respected the rules but was innovative enough to work around them when necessary. I'd sneak treats into my bedroom and lock myself away for hours. A good book plus a good treat equaled a good life.

I found everything outside of my immediate purview as something exotic that I needed to absorb. My home life was so structured and safe that anything different was a foreign experience. I clung to every opportunity for adventure with a white-knuckled grip. I feared even then that I might be too prone to naughtiness and disruption, and I hoped that if I encountered it, I'd be like Mrs. Piggle Wiggle and discipline myself with warmth and understanding and a dash of magic. I was young and naive, and everything in my life was like a novel unfolding with equal parts romance and main-character energy.

I never considered myself to be a Daddy's Girl, but I liked the way it sounded when people asked, so I usually replied that I was. I suppose I was a Daddy's Girl in some ways simply because I treasured time with him more than with my mom. He worked at an office all day while my mom stayed home and took care of me and my five siblings. I could count on seeing my mom from sunup to sundown—she was the one that took me school, to the doctor, to piano lessons, to all my church and extracurricular activities. And even though my dad seemed to be more involved and participatory than other dads I knew, it was still always expected for my mom to be there, but when my dad showed up, it was like a special guest appearance.

My dad was the life of the party, the guy everyone thought was their best friend. He had theories about everything, but he didn't force them down your throat or drone on and on unnecessarily. His theories were fascinating and useful. He taught us about his favorite pioneer hymns and inspired us to find God in nature. He also taught us about wilderness survival and how to white water raft. His life hacks were impossible to forget. My dad taught me that even when it was wet, a wool sweater would keep you warm; and if I ever got lost or separated from the group, to find a landmark or a water source and stay put. He would find me, and he wouldn't stop looking until he did. He believed that the best food and company could always be found at a local hole-in-the-wall restaurant, and that everywhere you go there is an opportunity to make a friend.

As a dad, he was responsible for all the typical "dad things": yard work, Sunday dishes, and most importantly road trips. He was the captain, cruise director, and the conductor. But ultimately, when we hit the road, he was the chauffeur. Growing up as a family of eight, we rarely flew on an airplane. Our vacations were limited mostly to long haul road trips from Colorado to Utah and back again for white-water rafting adventures and family reunions. My dad was one of the greatest long-distance drivers to have ever lived. He took a lot of pride in his efficiency and seemed to love being behind the wheel, and I never grew tired of road tripping with him.

His strategy on our trips was to leave before the crack of dawn under a blanket of darkness. We would load into the car groggy but excited, with our pillows and car bags that my mom had prepared full of snacks, games, and activities. Even though she had packed enough supplies to get us a few hundred miles, my dad had a routine he liked to follow. Right before we got on the interstate, he would make a stop at the 7-Eleven and buy us all a Hostess pie and a milk.

Watching him walk briskly back to our car with the sun creeping over the mountains and a plastic bag heavy with pies and chocolate milk was as exciting as spying Santa Claus himself with a sack full of toys. These extra provisions were a bribe. We all knew what was at stake. It was important to make as few stops as possible on the journey. Nothing crunched away at his driving time more than lingering bathroom breaks and loitering children begging him to buy them gas-station concessions. We'd load up and hit the road for as long as humanly possible before our bladders betrayed us. And by bladders, I mean specifically only mine and my sisters'. We would only stop for the girls to go, while boys on these road trips were trained to pee in the empty milk bottles and to do so with precision.

"The secret to making good time," Dad would say, while we coasted in the center lane at a respectable speed, "is to find a pigeon."

I began to scan the blurry countryside for a bird I feared I would only be able to recognize if it were in a flock on the steps of St. Paul's. And even then, it would need to be accompanied by Mary Poppins and a tuppence worth of bread crumbs.

My dad could tell I didn't understand.

"No," he explained with a laugh. "It's not that kind of pigeon. Our pigeon isn't an *actual* bird. It's a car."

He went on to explain that we were looking for a fellow traveler that was speeding. By trailing them at just the right distance, we could also speed, but we'd have someone just slightly ahead of us to get the ticket in case there was a speed trap along the route. Satisfied with his explanation, we continued along steadily in the center lane and waited patiently.

"Here we go, here we go," he would say excitedly, looking in the rearview mirror.

And sure enough a car, not a bird, would come speeding along in the fast lane to the left of us, flouting any posted speed limits or air surveillance warnings.

My dad would wriggle and hitch up in the driver's seat, gripping the top of the steering wheel with anticipation, and watch the pigeon speed by. Immediately, he'd click his blinker and accelerate on the gas to cross over into the fast lane.

"Coooooo, Coooooo," he would trill. "Looks like we got ourselves a pigeon. This guy will blaze the trail for us, and if there are any patrol cars lying in wait, they will nab him for speeding first while we tap the brakes and slow down just in time. Let *him* get the ticket."

Sure enough, it worked. It worked amazingly well, in fact. So well that I felt compelled to wonder why we called the sacrificial car a pigeon and not just a *patsy*. As soon as we spotted the cop along the side of the road, the pigeon would have too much speed to stop in time. But not us. We were at a safe enough distance to retreat, slow down, and scrape by unscathed. My dad would casually coast back into the center lane at a reduced speed, and we'd crane our necks to watch the police activity until the flashing lights faded into the distance.

One summer, my brother made the Little League All-Star team and everyone in my family was overjoyed at the accomplishment. I wasn't sure what it meant in terms of status or athletic ability, because all that was overlooked by the fact that making the A-team meant we were going on a family vacation: his team had been invited to attend a baseball tournament in California. And California meant a road trip. If his team placed in the tournament there was a chance we would get to go to the Little League World Series in Pennsylvania, which meant a second road trip, traveling transcontinental.

California was farther than we had ever driven before, and when weighing the costs of flying versus driving, it seemed driving was the only way to go. The added distance made it an even grander adventure, and my dad was challenged with figuring out how best to accommodate six kids with overactive bladders without damaging his own personal road trip record. Back in the days before Waze and MapQuest, the first thing people asked you upon arrival at your destination was how long the trip took: "Did you make good time?" they would ask before even saying hello. My dad found great pride in impressing relatives far and wide with his stunning statistics way before the computer estimated your ETA: "We made it in just under eight hours; only two bathroom breaks." Back pats and congratulations abounded. We, as his children, overheard these conversations and shared a sense of pride. I knew never to utter the dreaded words "Are we there yet?" even if the hours seemed to be dragging on. I imagined the trek to California would take some time, and I vowed to do my part. I would be the kind of kid my dad could count on, even if it meant my bladder would burst.

Eventually, my parents sat us down to reveal the solution to our long-distance road trip: we were renting a Winnebago.

I had no idea what a Winnebago was, but from the way my parents were talking, I knew to act excited. After cheering enthusiastically, I asked innocently, "What is a Winnebago?" My mom explained, "It's a car with a little house attached to it. You're going to be able to eat and sleep and watch movies and go to the bathroom and we will never even have to pull over. Dad will be able to drive straight through!"

I saw my dad's face cloud over with concern. This was the first time he realized what the Winnebago meant for him. He would be the only one driving. And I saw him do the math for the twenty-three hour distance. None of us had ever considered his need for food or a bathroom break. "Don't worry, Dad! You can do it!" we encouraged. And we actually believed he could.

The idea of a car with a house attached to it was more than I could imagine. I conjured up a Shel Silverstein illustration in my mind of the hybrid beast. A tiny house with one round window, perched on twelve wheels, that advanced like a tank and was able to leave the paved roads and travel onto the greenbelts of suburbia.

The night before we left for our road trip, the Winnebago was parked, solid and shining in our driveway, and we begged our parents to let us sleep in it: "That way you can leave as early as you want to and we won't have to wake up!" we suggested. But they were too wise to waste precious Winnebago time before it was necessary. After a brief tour of the outside, we were relegated back to our un-wheeled, un-moveable basic beds, unable to sleep with all the anticipation.

Loading into the Winnebago the next morning exceeded all of our expectations. There was a tiny spigot shower right over a tiny toilet bowl in a tiny bathroom. An accordion screen separated the bathroom from the galley where we had a sink and cupboards and a stovetop to cook on. It was a miniature kitchen where my mom could make us Kraft mac and cheese as we sailed down the interstate on our way to the promised land. There were bunk beds for the kids and a bedroom for the parents, which we immediately took over. We didn't count on them ever actually sleeping in it since they would be in the captain chairs at the front, driving this magical wonder. There was a table and a bench where we could play board games and color in our coloring books while Mom cooked and cleaned and Dad drove. I couldn't imagine a happier home or a happier family.

If you had told me then that I would be able to travel as an adult to lands farther and wider than the Winnebago could've taken me, I wouldn't have believed you and I wouldn't have cared. Because even now, after having traveled to Switzerland, Norway, Thailand, Qatar, so many corners of the world—nothing has left an impression on me like the feeling I had when I climbed up the four-rung ladder of our little car-house and crawled into the space perched above the driver's cab of the Winnebago. My enraptured face peering out the window watching a ribbon of highway expand in front of me while my entire world traveled safely along beneath me.

We were going to California, my birthplace and my birthright, so the trip felt like it belonged to me more than anyone else. I was born in Carmel-by-the-Sea, the third child and second daughter, while my dad was studying Russian at the Defense Language Institute in Monterey, California. This was on the job training for his career as a federal agent specializing in espionage. Because my dad had worked for the FBI, he relocated the family every two years, resulting in six children with five different birthplaces. My older sister was born in Salt Lake City, my brother in Minnesota, a sister in Texas, and two younger brothers in Denver, Colorado. But I, the blessed middle child, was born in the Golden State of Californ-I-A. And not only California, but Carmel-by-the-Sea, where Clint Eastwood was mayor!

We were headed to the land of sunshine, surfers, and celebrities. I had heard of Hollywood, but the place we were going to sounded much more exotic. I was pretty sure it would be swimming with stars! I mean, the name said it all: we were going to an *All-Star* Tournament? This wasn't a place for just regular baseball games, it was a place only worthy of the best of the best.

We were going to San Bernardino.

San Bernardino—the ill-reputed king of the inland empire. And if you had told me back then that it was known for its pollution and crime, I wouldn't have cared. It might as well have been Turks and Caicos to my untraveled soul. I loved the name. It rolled off my tongue. I pranced around and told anyone who would listen, "We're going to San Bernardino in a Winnebago." How could any girl be so lucky?

We bounded down the road like we were a World Series team on the winning bus! My mom bought us all matching outfits in his team's colors—bright royal blue and sunshine yellow. We were a sports family, and this was our greatest hour—to be a part of a traveling team, to be a part of a tournament, to be able to spend a week in blessed San Bernardino.

I loved baseball games! I loved being a part of the process: cheering, booing, hoping, praying, marking the scorecards, shagging the fly balls. But most of all, above everything else, I loved baseball games because I loved the Snack Shack.

The Snack Shack was like a pretend general store where every candy I had ever imagined was laid out and labeled at obscenely affordable prices. No tax, no math, no calculations, no embarrassing mishaps at the cash register. The Snack Shack spared customers the kind of humiliation that comes when you try to buy the clearly labeled $.99 Little Debbie Swiss Rolls and the cashier looks down at you demanding $1.06 when all you have is four measly quarters. The Snack Shack was a safe space where the change I siphoned from my dad's dresser drawer was welcomed and valued. It was usually staffed by older siblings or parents who never called attention to my multiple visits, my paying in pennies, or my endless desire for the long-lasting, yellow-tinged Astro Pop that was shaped like the lead of a sharpened pencil.

I was always most interested in the candy. Child-sized and packaged perfectly, the rows of candy reminded me of playing house and grocery store with my dolls, except these paper boxes were never empty. They contained multitudes. The Red Hots, the Lemonheads, the Boston Baked Beans. The chalky pastel Smarties on plastic white sticks, endless wrappers full of Bazooka Joe and Double Bubble gum. And always always always the daddy of Little League snacks: the Big League Chew. I would stuff my mouth with the shredded gum and chomp away until my jaw ached.

And this just covered Snack Shacks in Colorado; now we were going to a Snack Shack in *California*! On a tournament level! My candy-loving heart could only imagine what kind of sweet treasures existed beyond state lines!

I had never been to one, but I was already pretty sure that I loved baseball tournaments too. My brother's games were a chance to watch my dad in action. If he wasn't coaching, I'd sit close to him on the bleachers and ask him to explain what was happening on the field. He taught me to read the hand signals of the baseline coaches and to anticipate when someone was going to bunt. He even took time to explain why a pitcher would intentionally walk a batter, which I never really could wrap my head around.

When my dad grew tired of my incessant questions, he always found a way to keep me busy with the scorecards. He patiently taught me to fill out each one and explained that it was very important for me to get it right and not miss anything. I took my job very seriously. I mastered the meaning behind the tiny hieroglyphics and carefully advanced each of my batters, coloring in the tiny diamonds when they scored and reluctantly recording the letter K when they struck out. I held my breath whenever a pop fly went sailing in my brother's direction, and I felt the cloud of angst that came over our entire family whenever he was up to bat.

If God truly answered any of my prayers, every at-bat for my brother would have been a home run. I felt intense pressure for him to always do well, and for our team to always win. Our entire family's mood was dictated by their win-loss record. My brother always seemed satisfied with a solid base hit—looking back, he was probably just happy to not strike out to avoid the obvious disappointment on all of our faces. We had no concept of pressuring the player as a *bad* thing. This was how we showed we cared! We'd collectively groan if he swung and missed and shout out, "Keep your eye on the ball!" If he got called out at first, we'd storm off and shake our heads in disappointment. We considered ourselves a part of the team, and if we didn't care about each play, how could we expect the players to?

The baseball games filled our seven days in San Bernardino, but it was the nights that I remember the most. Once we returned to our motel, we were left to run about the premises with the other baseball families and sibling supporters. We were a band of brothers celebrating after a long day of being cooped up in the stands by running wild in the motel parking lot by night. We were in a concrete paradise where the Holiday Inn's fluorescent lighting made our eyes glow, and the parking lot lanterns lit our way.

After the sun set each evening, the frogs came out. We weren't sure where they came from, but I remembered hearing in Sunday School about a plague of frogs in the Bible, so I assumed that these frogs were also biblical in nature. First came the sounds of their tiny chirps and chortles. Then, as if on command, they would emerge from the shadows and begin their frantic journey to the pool. Thousands of tiny, green, perfectly formed miniature frogs. No bigger than a quarter. Most about the size of a nickel. Some as tiny as a dime. They would charge in hordes to our little round motel pool and we couldn't gather them up quickly enough. They seemed to leap in slow motion. Never before had I imagined I'd be able to capture wildlife like this *in* the wild. San Bernadino was fucking amazing!

I burst into our hotel room with a tiny quivering frog clasped in my hands and shouted for my parents to come and see. My mom recoiled: "Oh, get it out of here! Where did you find that?" She gently pushed me out of the door, closing it behind her, but not before I could hear her mutter under her breath, "This place is a dump."

A dump? I was stunned. What did she mean? This place was pure magic! How could she not see it? How could she not see that I had instantly become a member of the Swiss Family Robinson exploring a new land? This trip had transformed me from a chubby child chasing terrified frogs into a great explorer. I was holding a *frog* in my *bare hands*. Was that not in itself a tiny miracle? My soul was expanding, and I was doing things I'd never done before. Best of all, I was still safe and surrounded by my family. I was experiencing things for myself for the very first time, instead of just imagining them or reading about them in a book. Mrs. Piggle Wiggle could never! There was no forbidden gate or threshold I had to pass through in order to see the world. My house and everything I loved was attached to a car that would take me anywhere I wanted to go. My parents were my guides, my siblings were my built-in best friends, and the frogs were a thousand potential princes.

The tiny creak and croak of each froglet's persistent chirp called to me like a siren's song.

The drive home was more somber than the drive there. We spent the hours cleaning up and preparing the Winnebago of Dreams to be returned to the rental company. Our coloring books were filled, our board games were missing pieces, and the septic tank had begun to smell. We had been eliminated from the tournament prematurely, and there would be no extended trip to the Little League World Series in Pennsylvania. I tried to remember the feeling of joy we had when everything was full of excitement and anticipation and hope.

For weeks after we came home, I told anyone who crossed my path about the incredible land of San Bernardino. One day, after sharing the majesty of our family vacation with the guy bagging our groceries, my mom pulled me aside and said, "Heather, just say we went to *California*. You don't have to say the city. I know you loved it, but San Bernardino isn't cool."

FOUR

MISS KELLY KIRK

When I first met my third-grade teacher, she had straight, shiny brown hair with pageboy bangs that framed her face. She wore white Peter Pan–collared shirts underneath puffed-sleeve sweaters with knitted rows of hearts and ducks and sailboats across her chest. Her shoes were decidedly trendy—soft-soled leather moccasins with fringe and leather ties. They were all the rage in the mid-'80s and, honestly, felt like kind of a waste for *just* a teacher.

Shortly after the school year began, my mom signed me up for extracurricular macramé classes in Miss Kirk's apartment. She said it was "to help her out with a little extra money." But the real reason we paid the ticket price was obvious to me: being able to enter into a teacher's world—into her natural habitat *and* to be taught a handicraft? This was better than a trip to Disneyland! It was worth every penny.

Miss Kirk lived in a small walk-up apartment in Denver. It was the first time I had ever seen an apartment building in real life. Everyone I knew lived in pastel stuccoed suburban houses, one of six models available in the planned development surrounding our elementary school. Our lives were organized around marriage and family and our homes.

"I hate the thought of her living there all alone," my mom would say wistfully. "I wish she could find a nice man to marry."

I knew *we* were in no position to find her a man. All the nice men we knew were spoken for by *our* kind: Mormons. And we only set Mormons up with other Mormons. But we pined for others to aspire to our same standards of hearth and home. As nice and as pretty as Miss Kirk was, she was not an option for anyone we knew unless she was willing to get baptized and join the church. But we still wanted the best for her. We didn't know what faith she practiced, we just knew she wasn't one of us.

So all we could hope for Miss Kelly Kirk was to have any man, regardless of his religious background, willing to take her on. In the meantime, it was clear to my eight-year-old self that the least we could do was to throw a little macramé money her way so that she could keep herself up. We were doing our part to ensure that she didn't let herself go and trade in her trendy moccasins for sensible topsiders and eventually orthopedics.

And then came the stuff of urban legend: the sixth-grade teacher Mr. Sanders had a brother—an eligible, non-Mormon brother—to set up with Miss Kirk. When my mom heard the news, she let out a whoop and excitedly informed me of this new development. I didn't understand her glee. What would this mean for me and her other third-grade students? We liked Miss Kirk exactly the way she was: single, dedicated, and offering extracurricular craft classes on the weekends.

My mom kept tabs on all the proceedings, and the reports came back quickly that the first date went great, and the two were dating.

Now, whenever we went to Miss Kirk's apartment, my mom asked me if I noticed anything different. Was there a new lightness in her macrame-twisting hands? A bit more joy in her instruction? When I obliged that she did in fact seem happier, my mom was ecstatic. Hope was not lost. She was getting out of here. Sayonara spinsterhood!

I was panicked for Miss Kirk to go anywhere, but my mom assured me that she would still stay on as a teacher. ("Probably just for a year or two at most," my mom explained. "Once she's married, I'm sure she'll be anxious to start a family.") It seemed clear to me that this whole teaching thing was just what she had to do to provide for herself, but now she had a *man*. And regardless of who he was or what he was providing, everyone acted like it would be better than whatever Miss Kirk had going alone.

The wedding came and went, and I was disappointingly not asked to be a flower girl. I felt robbed, but still pretended to be supportive. The big moment, of course, came when the students walked into Miss Kirk's classroom the following Monday and saw her new identity. You could see where Miss Kirk had been erased and replaced with clean, crisp print across the chalkboard: "Mrs. Sanders."

The big "Mrs." and the husband's last name—Sanders—wiped away any trace of Miss Kirk's side gigs and singledom. Her former life had vanished with one swipe of the eraser. When I proudly showed my friends my new macramé plant holders, I had to correct myself every time: "I made them with Miss Kir—I mean, *Mrs.* Sanders. She used to have classes at her house . . . I mean, apartment, before she got married."

While I instinctively felt a strange pride announcing that she had gotten married, I also felt a strange sadness about how easily her old identity had been replaced. Miss Kirk had been my entire world. She'd seemed happy and fulfilled to me. She had a ceramic frog collection that she displayed on shelves around the classroom and that we were careful not to touch or mess with. Her hair was shiny and her smile was kind, and I never detected a hint of sadness or despair or longing behind her eyes. It wasn't until my mom pointed out that she was alone and I sensed pity in her voice that I realized I might not be reading Miss Kirk's situation correctly. Her own apartment, her beaded moccasins, her macramé side hustle . . . this was a woman thriving, not a woman pining. Why was my mom fronting so hard that we needed to help her? Wasn't Miss Kirk the one helping us? I didn't get the chance to ask the questions because it all seemed so inevitable. This was not presented to be anything other than the way it was: the facts of life for women. So I took note. And I shifted the way I saw Mrs. Sanders and all of her accomplishments.

She didn't waste a minute wiping her old name off the chalkboard and proudly displaying her new one. Was it a romantic gesture, or confirmation that Miss Kirk had given herself an upgrade? Why would anyone be that anxious to shed their old identity and take on a new, unproven one? Didn't she love us, love teaching, love ceramic frogs and and macrame? Or had she been faking all of it, just biding time until she could replace her own passions with the passions of her husband and her children? That was the message I understood. Anything we do for ourselves as young women is just preparation for the identities we will later adopt as wives and mothers. Our single selves need to be disposable, so it's best not to invest too much in them. In order for a traditional marriage to work, the math has to add up so it doesn't make sense to add a lot of numbers that you'll eventually just have to subtract. The goal is to make sure you don't overstep the boundary by becoming anything too immovable or important to give up. We strive to become overly qualified but not overly ambitious; becoming *just enough* to get to change your name on the chalkboard. Whatever it takes to get to the MRS. of it all.

"Miss" to "Mrs." without a stopover at "Ms." Forty years ago, so much was contained in those tiny declarations. Available, Taken, and I'll Never Tell.

I learned more about these distinctions and the weight they each carried in eighth grade when a watch I purchased gave out a mere six weeks after I bought it. I had ordered it through mail-order submission at the back of a magazine, right below the ad for the Columbia Records CD subscription club. There was no physical store to return it to. All I could find was a tiny address written in the fine print of the paper insert folded neatly inside the watch's plastic package. I was so distraught and felt like a fool having wasted forty dollars on a watch that was a piece of junk. They had sold me on a false bill of goods, and I refused to accept it. I wrote a letter to the company address, explaining how my newly purchased watch had stopped working and how I wanted something to be done about it. When I went to sign the letter, my mom stepped in.

"Sign it with a 'Ms.' rather than 'Miss.' It's more powerful. It will keep them guessing. They won't know you're just a young, single fourteen-year-old with a sense of entitlement. 'Ms.' can mean single or married." If that was the case, I thought, why not just use it all the time? But she was right. It worked. The company sent a replacement watch and apologized to the mysterious Ms. Deans for the time and inconvenience.

Despite the fact that it worked, the one variable I couldn't quite shake was the unchanging, steadfast nature of "Mr." In terms of leverage and mystery, "Mr." seemed like the most powerful of all the titles.

"Mr." was clearly not available to me as a woman, so the next best thing would have to be a "Mr(s)." The power was all in the R.

Life was teaching me, slowly but surely, that Mrs. was the best one available to me because it carried more weight than mystery. It carried more respect, more distinction, more success than any possibility or allure of singledom ever could. Sure, Ms. was more intriguing than Miss, but it couldn't hold a candle to Mrs. You can think you're being mysterious with a Ms. at the front of your name, but the smart ones know that if you can lead with Mrs., you do.

Mrs. was so powerful, in fact, that it could replace your entire name and identity. Once I got married, mail came to the house addressed to Mr. and Mrs. Frank William Gay III. I didn't even need my own name anymore, much less my own address, credit score, or utility bill now that I was married. That's how powerful Mrs. was to me. It was shorthand for "whoever I was before doesn't matter anymore."

Miss Kirk was only twenty-three, a far cry from being a spinster. But that didn't prevent the shadow of it all from looming over her head. Spinsters were the unspoken tragedy of an unmarried woman, destined to sit at a spinning wheel, making yarn until the cobwebs grew so thick they became ghosts. I never saw a spinning wheel at Miss Kirk's apartment, but I knew what they looked like because my mom had an antique one as decorative furniture in our house. It was old and spindly and missing the foot pedals and bobbin, but we never noticed. None of that mattered to us. We would use our hand to manually spin the wheel, sit on the matching stool and let our imaginations weave a tapestry. We turned that spinning wheel into the helm of a mighty ship, into a smoky roulette wheel in an old-timey casino, and a medieval torture device when we had enough yarn to tie each other up. We reenacted over and over the scene from *Sleeping Beauty* where the princess pricks her finger, walking like zombies in a trance until we jabbed our hands on the imaginary needle. The spinning wheel represented everything imaginative about childhood play. I never once considered it to be a symbol of loneliness or unfulfillment or drudgery. It was a magnificent tool, and in the right hands, it could be turned into anything.

Miss Kirk could've been the right hands to do it. She was the type of spinster I would want to be. But the world was set on spinning her single life into a cautionary tale rather than a great destiny, and her classroom courtship into a success story of a woman being rescued from herself.

The truth is, a lot of the women I look up to are the kinds of women that the world would describe as spinsters. The women I want to be like are goddamn cheetahs: pioneers who have traded their dog-eared copies of Dr. Laura Schlessinger's *The Proper Care and Feeding of Husbands* for a coffee-stained, heavily annotated copy of Glennon Doyle's *Untamed*. Accomplished, ambitious women breaking glass ceilings and decades of tradition by redefining what it means to be a woman outside of being a wife and mother.

Spinsters are women who turn straw into gold. They take the words of doubt and insecurity that the world throws upon them and turn them into something entirely different. There is an aching for the person I was before I became who I thought I was supposed to be. And there is no doubt that the sacrifices we make as women require us to spin the narrative in order to take the sting out of all the martyrdom. Maybe it is just the plight of all women to fear that we have squandered our best selves in service to those we love the most.

Miss Kelly Kirk became Mrs. Sanders, and just like her name, her life was never the same. And I hope and pray it was immeasurably better. I lost track of her once my family moved to Utah in the ninth grade, but I choose to believe that she got everything she ever wanted. I just hope that she continued crafting her homemade plant holders and taught her own kids to macramé.

In that tiny sliver of time when she was for herself and for us, her third-grade students, she shaped my life in ways that she likely would never believe. Even though society wanted to take her off the shelf, I'm grateful that she put herself on it for me, even if just for a moment.

FIVE

WEE WETTER

A lot of people think it's hard to keep a secret, but when you have something about yourself you want to hide, or something about yourself that you don't understand, keeping a secret can be amazingly easy. If there is enough shame, you'll never share. And when it comes to sacred family secrets, we tell ourselves that our silence is about nobility or integrity, but really it's more about survival and fear.

Keeping secrets has always been a part of my life. I can't remember a time when I didn't feel like I had something to hide, something to be ashamed of, something that I understood could never be shared with anyone. Because if I did reveal my secret, I'd have to admit to myself that it was real and that I was different.

I was a chronic bedwetter. From toddler to teenager, I wet the bed every night—right as rain, if you will. Each morning, I woke up with a secret in a situation that I couldn't understand, that I had to cover up, and that I couldn't change no matter how hard I tried.

When it became clear that it was becoming a problem, my mom addressed the issue with fervor. She took me to a therapist, afraid that bedwetting was a symptom of molestation or abuse. Bedwetting seemed manageable, but her bigger fear was that this little habit was a symptom of a darker, even more unspeakable problem. When that was ruled out, she took me to a urologist, to determine if there was a medical explanation. She researched hypnotherapy and tough love, punishment and reward, but nothing seemed to work. My bladder hadn't betrayed me on long haul road trips, but the second I fell asleep, I lost all control. Bedwetting seemed to be embedded into my DNA.

What my parents had privately struggled with soon became a situation involving the entire family. It occurred to them that perhaps having a companion in bed might cure me of what many experts claimed was merely a "bad habit." The theory was that another person next to me would keep my sleep restless enough and my shame deep enough to keep me dry. So they volunteered each sibling one by one. This was my brothers' and sisters' first introduction to me as a bedwetter. And it was a violent one. Especially because of the ruse of it all. My parents set up the experiment under the guise of what felt like an indulgence—a feigned sleepover on a school night. It started out all giggles and smiles as we crawled under the covers, only for them to be woken up in the middle of the night in a pool of wet. They didn't know if the ship was going down or if they were slowly bleeding out. It was a nightmare made real. And I, the offender, was unable to comfort or explain away their trauma because I was sleeping soundly bathed in my own.

I was hard to rouse, but if the dampness eventually woke me up, it lasted only long enough for me, in my sleep-soaked haze, to scoot away from the wet spot. Sometimes, the wet spot could not be avoided. In that case, I would strip myself of my wet pajamas and stumble toward the linen closet to grab the nearest towel, thick duvet, or cherished handmade quilt to create a dry barrier upon which to fall immediately back to sleep on.

The bedding method was yet another tactic employed by my sleep-deprived parents. One afternoon, I came home from school only to find that my mom had redecorated my room with matching sheets, accent pillows, curtains, and lampshades. I came into my room with a sense of awe, shock, and and low-grade anxiety. I loved it, but the extreme room makeover seemed out of the blue. It wasn't my birthday; it wasn't back to school. There was no fathomable reason I could think of to deserve such a surprise, and it made me nervous. I knew my parents, and in a family with six kids, this type of blatant favoritism did not go unquestioned. There had to be strings attached.

As I walked around the room ruching the ruffle borders of the little pillows and pulling back the gauzy matching curtains, my mom interrupted my daydream with an explanation: "Maybe with beautiful new bedding, you'll feel less inclined to soil it."

Ah. The *reason*. My mom thought, in my sleep-soaked haze, that I would have enough respect for these linens that I would keep them dry. But she was wrong. I was no bedding elitist! Had she not noticed I had wet the bed on blankets thick and thin, and bunk beds top and bottom? I left no stone unturned, no linen unspotted. My bladder did not check for thread counts or "dry clean only" instructions. I simply fell asleep and didn't wake up come hell or, well, high water.

But this new bedding came with an added level of security. And my mom was hoping the matching curtains would soften the blow. It was called the Wee Wetter alarm, and it was the last resort.

Conventional wisdom of the day was that bedwetters were lazy sleepers that had developed a bad habit, and by interrupting their sleep pattern at the precise moment, you could retrain their brain and cure them. My parents read about the theory and at first tried doing it manually. They estimated that I seemed to be wetting the bed sometime between midnight and 2:00 a.m., so they took turns going into my room, waking me up, and walking me to the bathroom. Their efforts failed miserably. I was incredibly hard to wake up. And even when I appeared to be awake, I really wasn't. It was more of a sleepwalking stupor. They realized this one night when they turned away for a moment, only to discover me crouching down in the walk-in closet, unaware that I wasn't across the hall in the bathroom. Worse still was when they would wake up in the middle of the night only to discover that they were a few minutes too late, or a few minutes too early, and that interrupting my sleep pattern was not solving the problem but merely interrupting their own. That's when they decided to go automatic and splurge on a modern device like the Wee Wetter alarm.

Advertised in department store catalogs and nationally syndicated advice columns, the Wee Wetter employed the tactics of classical conditioning to night-train deep-sleeping bladders. I can imagine my mother, sleep-interrupted and bone-weary, stumbling across an advice column where another distraught mother sought guidance with the same dampened spirit.

Ann Landers was a well-known advocate for bedwetters. She brought awareness to the issue she described as a deep, dark family secret that riddled its victims with shame and low self-esteem. She gave lots of advice, ranging from educational programs to increased compassion, but the column finally caught my mom's eye when it suggested a battery alarm device that one could purchase from the Sears catalog.

The Wee Wetter alarm appeared to be a godsend. It consisted of a small metal box with wires attached to a moisture sensitive pad. The alarm featured a grooved dial allowing for a range of volume from one to twenty. The dial controlled the volume of the alarm triggered by the detection of moisture anywhere on the sensory pad that was placed just underneath the mattress's fitted sheet. When the first drops of urine hit the sensitive pad, a child who had just started to pee would, in theory, be awakened by the squelching alarm just in time to stop midstream, get up, and walk to the bathroom. What sounded reasonable in theory was much more difficult in practice. The bladder control alone was improbable, and that was without considering that it would also have to be performed in the middle of the night, in pitch-black darkness, under duress. And under duress was the only way you could experience the ear-shattering sounds of the Wee Wetter.

"BEEP BEEP BEEP BEEP!"

The alarm would rage on relentlessly from the first droplet until it was turned off or unplugged. And the time frame from first drop-let to full tropical storm was less than fifteen seconds. I never stood a chance. I got to know the sound all too well—not because it ever actually worked or prevented any bedwetting, but because it rang continuously until my parents would tear into my room, their eyes burning and furious, yelling.

"WAKE UP! CAN'T YOU HEAR IT? HOW CAN YOU SLEEP THROUGH IT? FOR THE LOVE OF GOD, CHILD, WAKE UP!"

And I did wake up, not from the alarm, but from their voices when they screamed at me. At that point, the alarm had already woken up everyone on our street *except* for me. I lay there in a symphony of sound, blissfully unaware, dreaming of a relaxing float in an idyllic natural hot spring.

"Huh? Hear what? Oh! I can hear it now that I'm awake. I couldn't hear it before because I was sleeping."

What did other people do while they slept? Keep one eye on the door, one eye on their bladder, and a third eye on their to-do list should insomnia strike? When my eyes were closed, I was off to dreamland, and I couldn't be bothered with mundane tasks as basic as bodily functions. How declassé! I was young, I was dreaming, and I still believed that nothing should or could interrupt my dreams, especially not the ear-splitting screams of the Wee Wetter alarm or my defeated parents.

I didn't wet the bed out of spite or pain, and no therapist or medicine or alarm system could get me to stop. It was all just a matter of biology, a matter of how my specific brain worked with the sensors in my specific body. Maybe this was the deal with the Devil that I had to make in order to memorize every state capital and the entire song book of *The Sound of Music*. Maybe it was just who I was. And sure it was inconvenient and embarrassing and different from the behavior of every kid in my family *and* America, but I couldn't change it if I tried.

One time, at a sleepover that I begged my mom to let me go on despite her misgivings, I woke up to a wet sleeping bag and had to think quickly. I jumped up, grabbed a cup, and pretended that I had spilled a glass of water on myself in the middle of the night. I'm not sure if anyone caught on, but if they did, they didn't say it to my face. The last thing I needed was for a friend to discover my bedwetting only to return to school the next day and tell everyone in class about it.

It was my mom's greatest fear too, and she tried to protect me as as best she could. But this was the '80s. Everything was about conformity and assimilation and being normal. We all dressed the same, listened to the same music, and talked the same even though we knew we were different. We tried our best to fit in. There was no support group, no community, no network of friends to get together with and talk about our common problem. It's not like she could visit my class and explain to them, "Hi, this is Heather. And although you might not be able to tell it from looking at her, she suffers from a condition called enuresis. That may sound like a fancy medical word to you and me, but really it just means that the way she sleeps and the way you sleep are a little bit different. It's nothing to worry about. Her nights are just noticeably less dry and require much more laundry than other kids. You'll see that, despite not being able to go to slumber parties or have liquids after 8:00 p.m., she's just like you and me. So there's no reason to be afraid of her."

I would've loved for that to have happened. Imagine a slumber party with Big Gulps after midnight and a room full of rubber sheets! Whether you're fourteen or forty, when you find out there are others like you, it's the biggest comfort in the world. Michael Landon wrote and directed a made-for-television film about growing up as a bedwetter called *The Loneliest Runner*. And as far as I'm concerned, it's more moving than *Chariots of* fucking *Fire*. Now, when I read about someone famous being a bedwetter as a child, I feel an immediate kinship. If I ever ran into Sarah Silverman, I wouldn't want to talk to her about any of her celebrity experiences. I'd want to talk to her about bedwetting. Did she ever get exposed? Did her parents buy her a Wee Wetter too?

Despite its initial ineffectiveness, my mom still held out high hopes for the alarm. When the initial test runs failed to work, she resigned to placing the pad on top of the fitted sheet, realizing that changing the waterproof pad was a lot easier than changing everything else. And thus the Wee Wetter persisted with a slight adaptation.

If I had a friend coming over, I was careful to hide the alarm under a pillow and the pad under a blanket, making sure that no cords were loose or dangling. The fear of being caught kept me on high alert. I had something to hide, and my secret had to be protected at all costs.

I must've grown comfortable or forgetful on the fateful day that I invited Emily Schneider over without first burying the alarm deep within the pillows.

Emily was one of my best friends at Homestead Elementary School, which meant that I couldn't tell her any of my actual family secrets. Every day for lunch, she brought mini, chewy bagels and silver-dollar-sized slices of salami. I didn't even like the look or taste of salami, but when Emily ate her sandwiches, they looked like the chicest and coolest lunches in the world compared to my peanut butter and jelly on wheat bread. She was Episcopalian, and she let me know in first grade that she was a Democrat, to which I proudly replied, "That's so interesting! I'm a Mormon."

I was so excited about my bedroom makeover that I let down my guard. As soon as she entered the room, she walked over to the nightstand and innocently asked, "What's this?"

Following quickly behind her, I froze in shock to see Emily's hand painstakingly turning the ridged dial of my Wee Wetter alarm from one to twenty.

There it was, just sitting out in the open next to my designer lamp and battered copy of *Tuck Everlasting*. The brand name was proudly displayed in an arc above the dial. I thought about lunging forward and knocking it off the nightstand, but I was too far away, and she had already been observing it for too long. Time stood still as I watched her hand gently trace the cords leading from the box down to the mattress beside it. It was all happening in slow motion. There was no going back. I was about to be discovered. I needed to think of something, and I needed to think of something fast.

"Oh! That's my Wee Wetter!" I said too loudly, with enthusiasm, careful to cover the quivering fear in my voice.

I wasn't sure where to go next, but I knew I couldn't get around the name written in cursive on the alarm. What else could Wee Wetter mean? The words stumbled out of my mouth before I could even evaluate them: "I get really bad nosebleeds when the air is dry, so this alarm acts like a humidifier and it keeps the air around me moist during the night."

The previous week, our classmate Robert had interrupted our lesson on long division with a bloody nose. The entire class had laughed and jeered because everyone knows that spontaneous nosebloods don't just happen. They are caused by only one thing, and that's picking your nose! Our teacher had jumped in to defend him, explaining that we shouldn't make fun of Robert because nosebleeds were sometimes a natural consequence of dry air. Somehow, that precious new nugget of information had stayed with me. And now it was proving to be beyond useful.

Emily questioned how humidifying was possible with no water reservoir to be seen.

"Trust me, Emily, there's a water reservoir, and you're looking at her."

Emily was going to be tough to convince. Her parents were both pediatricians, and she had been the one to explain to me how sex worked earlier that year. Conversations about anatomy and reproduction were dinner table talk in her household, while my family kept such conversations to the stork delivering Baby Dumbo. She had grown frustrated when I couldn't understand how men ejaculated: "Is it intentional? Like peeing?" I wondered. I understood both voluntary and involuntary peeing, so either answer would've been acceptable. But she rolled her eyes at me and scoffed at my ignorance. Selling her on the Wee Wetter wasn't going to be easy, but I was mid-river now and there was no turning back.

"What does the dial do?" she asked.

"Oh, I just adjust it based on the level of moisture I need. If it's an especially dry night, I'll crank it up to twenty. Keeps me surrounded in a cloud of wet."

With a resigned shrug, she pretended to understand. Then her interest moved on to scanning my bookshelves, admiring the rows and rows of assorted paperbacks and well-placed tchotchkes. I had narrowly evaded exposure, but the humiliation remained hot and heavy in my chest.

It would be a few more years before I finally woke up dry consistently. And when I did, it felt like magic. Luckily, even if Emily caught on, she never revealed my deep dark secret. My mom was convinced that it was the hypnotherapy that finally fixed me. I would sit in a therapist's office, and he would describe, in a lulling voice, me walking through a beautiful field, coming upon a river, where I would see a gate that controlled a dam. I was the one in charge of the great iron wheel that both opened and shut the gate to allow the river of water through. The creative visualization involved me reaching down and turning the wheel of the gate and stopping the flow of water. We all hoped that my brain understood that this was not just hypnotherapy; it was also clearly a metaphor.

The real resolution to my bedwetting most likely just came with age. Once I grew up, the synapses in my brain miraculously began coordinating better with the impulses of my body, and I no longer lived under a cloud of shame or a cloud of wet.

Was it a pain to wet the bed every night? Yes. But the harder part was hiding it. Covering it up, waking up early enough to take a bath, hoping that my mom wouldn't come into my room, hoping that my siblings wouldn't tell their friends, hoping every morning that it would eventually stop and that I'd wake up free of it. After all, it was just a part of who I was, it wasn't all of who I was. A part I couldn't change even if I tried.

And by the time I was cured, I felt so much relief that it was hard to remember what it felt like to be filled with fear. I had not known the weight (or the wet) of it all until I finally felt the freedom.

SIX

TIJUANA

The annual senior trip for the students at Olympus High School in Holladay, Utah, was traditionally to Newport Beach, California. I'm not sure exactly when that tradition started, but every summer, immediately following graduation, all the seniors loaded up sleeping bags, pillows, and as much cash as we could muster and piled into our parents' eight-passenger Suburbans for the trek out west. Our parents were generous to a fault with their trust, their cash, and their possessions. We numbered close to twenty-five seniors with little to no real life experience, but we were armed with enough cars, hormones, and discretionary money to get ourselves into serious trouble if we tried. I had traveled with friends' families for a weekend here or there, but I'd never crossed three state lines, not to mention in a frenzied spirit of celebration. This was new territory. There was very little thought given to seat belts or oil checks or emergency roadside kits. Chaperones, rental contracts, and security deposits were the farthest thing from our minds.

We wanted excitement; we wanted to pretend to dance with danger. We were focused on freedom and fun and finally being *real* adults now that we had graduated from high school.

I was only seventeen when it came time for my senior trip, but I had been putting money aside for months, hoping to create enough of a cash stockpile for two main excursions: admission to the Six Flags Magic Mountain theme park and admission to a planned dinner at a fancy restaurant called Medieval Times. The restaurant had been described to me as a Renaissance castle where we would eat like actual serfs with no utensils and be entertained by jousting knights in shining armor. It sounded like a dream come true, combining all the things I loved: hearty handheld food, pageantry, cosplay, and competition. I didn't know if the men working there were hot or not, but imagining a man in a full blown suit of armor stirred my loins like nothing else had before.

The most exotic dining experience I'd had to date was at Casa Bonita, a novelty restaurant with cliff divers, caves, and quesadillas. The tables were situated in a makeshift rainforest where we ate kids' meals off partitioned plates and drank flat root beer from paper cups. We were titillated by mariachi bands and Black Bart's Cave. But the main attraction was the bronzed high divers in loincloths performing acrobatic cliff dives into tiny pools of water every hour on the hour. I always burned my tongue on the sopapillas they presented for dessert and remembered never wanting to eat the mushy gray-green peas that accompanied my chicken tenders. It had a distinct smell like hot grease and chlorine that smacked you in the face as soon as you walked through the doors of the pink stuccoed *palacio* and stepped into the Jurassic Park that was the restaurant. However, at Casa Bonita I never complained. It was fine dining like I had never known, and I had experienced the lemon chicken at Jade Garden.

This restaurant in California, Medieval Times, sounded like it was the first place that could measure up to Casa Bonita's impossibly high bar. It was an excursion I definitely didn't want to miss, and I was willing to pay whatever it took. Based on my friends' rough estimates, we believed that it would cost around thirty to forty dollars, which was a lot of money to me, but I was willing to spend it. The price of the meal was my only consideration. I gave no thought to tax, tip, transportation, gas, or parking. It never crossed my mind. I didn't have enough experience independent of my parents to have any concept of how those things worked in the real world.

Anyone staying in the rental house (at least officially) had to pay their share two weeks prior to our departure date. My parents had covered the cost of housing as a graduation gift and agreed that I could go so long as I covered my personal expenses and souvenirs. By the time it came down to final budgeting, my lodging had been covered, and I figured that aside from my two big-ticket items, the rest of the trip's costs would be covered by whatever linty cash remains I could scrounge up from my pockets.

I rode in my friend Brad's parents' Suburban. We listened to Garth Brooks and George Strait on repeat the entire drive. I was in what I lovingly refer to as my "country music phase." It was the early nineties, and country music had taken over the mainstream airwaves. I was almost eighteen, and this was my senior trip. I was seeing the world! I was going to Californ-I-A. I had visited parts of California before including the exotic San Bernardino, sure, but this trip felt distinctly different.

This time there were roller coasters and jousting knights on the itinerary with no adult supervision whatsoever. The imagined adventure enveloped me, and I was giddy.

I wanted to buy every souvenir I saw at every road stop along the way, but I hadn't brought enough money. My job as the lead employee at the Golden Spoon Frozen Yogurt paid $4.50 an hour, and even though I had worked at least twenty-five hours a week and had been eliminating all impulse purchases on matching sets from The Limited, I had only saved around four hundred dollars, and I needed to make it last. I hadn't created any budget for food, and I was hoping to survive off scraps and leftovers. Maybe I'd even lose a few pounds. Who needed food when you had sun and fun and most importantly, FREEDOM?

The house we rented was right on the sand in Newport Beach. It was a blush, stuccoed, three-story standard—barely discernible from its neighboring homes in vanilla and pale blue, a far cry from the bubblegum pink of Casa Bonita—with a nonexistent driveway and a one-and-a-half-foot cement barrier separating our back patio from the public boardwalk. It was exactly like every other beach house next to it. There weren't nearly enough beds, so everyone planned on sprawling out on the couches, floors, recliners, and carpets as necessary. There was to be no hooking up—at least not openly. This wasn't a trip about sex; this was a trip about wholesome adventure. Of course, people had "boyfriends" and "girlfriends," but we didn't call them that and there was an unspoken understanding that we weren't messing around. If we were, we weren't admitting it to ourselves or anyone else. We deluded ourselves in a world of "Don't ask, don't tell . . . but also it's not happening, so just don't ask."

When we signed the rental contract, we had put down that we

were seniors, strategically ignoring the fact that we weren't senior citizens but were instead seniors in high school. This was 1992, well before your social-media profiles were linked to your Airbnb contact. We could hide our youth behind our parents' credit card numbers and landlines. All we needed was one responsible adult to sign the rental contract, and as long as they didn't mention that we were planning to fit twenty-five seniors into a home that slept ten, we were covered. There were no Ring cameras or security footage to capture our arrival, so as soon as we pulled up in a caravan of SUVs, we hopped out as quickly and haphazardly as clowns from a clown car, hoping to distract the property managers.

The trip went by at breakneck speed. We'd wile away our days on the beach, and then at night try to coordinate dinner plans with twenty-five people arguing for the cheapest versus the closest versus the best option. When it came time for my special night, only half the group opted for the Medieval Times excursion—*fools!* I tried to convince them that they were missing out. Some complained that it was too far away and too expensive, but I pointed out that it was only twelve miles away on the map—a mere hop, skip, and a jump from Newport Beach to Anaheim. How long could it possibly take? An hour and a half later, as we sat creeping along in traffic, I had my answer: much longer than I thought. This would not be the last time I underestimated our driving time.

However, as soon as I walked through those laminate castle doors and caught a whiff of horse manure coupled with garlic mashed potatoes, the dark cloud of the preceding traffic vanished in front of my eyes. I knew I was in for a night of wonder. I affixed my paper crown to my head and never looked back. I was transported back in time, I ate with my hands, I cheered, I drank from a metal goblet. I truly lived. My knight didn't win, but the fact that I still remember that little fact proves to me that I was deeply invested not only in the joust itself, but in its ultimate outcome.

As we drove home from the restaurant in equally excruciating traffic, a group conversation erupted. A few friends asked if anyone wanted to travel down to San Diego or Tijuana to "buy authentic vanilla for our mothers and silver jewelry at dirt cheap prices." Weren't those the only reasons to go to Tijuana? My heart jumped! I sensed opportunity. The ones proposing the trip were *not* my church friends. They were my church adjacent friends, and they were known to be wild; one was even Greek. If there was going to be a chance to push any boundaries and dance on the dark side, this was it. There was enough of a cover and enough of an opportunity. I wanted to go desperately. But I had driven down to California with a different group of friends, and the driver had made it clear that he wanted to get an early start and head home right after checkout the following day. I expressed my dilemma and waited to see how the dust settled. We discovered that if I swapped places with Kelly, then I could leave Brad's Suburban and instead drive home with Katie Herman. Everyone in her car—minus Kelly—wanted to go to Tijuana. Kelly agreed, and so it was decided that I'd get to go to Tijuana with Katie and the gang and drive back to Utah later in the afternoon.

As planning progressed, Katie decided that she'd rather spend the day at the beach instead of in the car, so she wanted to hang out with Brad's group until they were forced to leave the rental. Then, she'd head to the beach and wait for us to come back from . . . Mexico. Checkout time was 12:00 sharp. We calculated that if we left the house around 8:00, we'd make it to Tijuana around 10:00 a.m. We'd spend an hour or so shopping and then head back to pick Katie up around 1:00 or 2:00 p.m. Our memory of all the time spent in California traffic just the day prior had clearly been long forgotten. We had a foldable map and immovable confidence. We were ready.

We were loose with travel times, traffic, and border crossing. None of us wore watches or had any sense of actual time. There were no cell phones, and communication between Newport Beach and Mexico was nearly impossible. We assumed that the worst-case scenario would be a strict property manager who was firm about the 12:00 checkout. We figured that Katie would be forced to "hang out" on the beach for a maximum of one to two hours until we arrived to pick her up. No big deal. It was the perfect plan! What could possibly go wrong?

I knew in the back of my mind that the timeline was tight, but I pushed the feeling down. I wasn't a decision maker on this excursion. I was a last-minute add-on, and I didn't feel any real desire to sabotage our trip by analyzing it any further. I had no idea how rental properties worked or how checkout times were enforced, and my heart was set on the foreign sojourn ahead, so I quieted my concerns and leaned on the expertise and enthusiasm of my friends.

When we left for Tijuana that morning, everyone else in the house was sound asleep with their clothing and belongings strewn every-where. I told myself there was no way they were going to be able to wake up, pack up, clean up, and be out of there by noon. I figured we might even get back in time to still use the house and shower before we headed out for the long drive home to Utah. This was my plan and, in my mind, it made perfect sense. Much like my budgeting, I figured the little details would just work themselves out.

Crossing the border into Mexico back then was less of a hassle than buying a latte at Starbucks today. We parked the car and casually strolled across the walkway, surrounded by a horde of other tourists, while a middle-aged guy in a border control uniform kicked back in his chair with a magazine and a donut. There was no checking of identification or inquiries about our plans in Mexico. Vendors approached us as soon as we crossed the line: little children pulling at my white cotton shorts shouting, "Sheek-lay! Sheek-lay!" while gesturing to their clutched boxes of Chiclet gum. This was my first footstep on foreign soil. Hearing children sell gum in their native Spanish made me feel, for the first time, like a citizen of the world. I found it incredibly moving. Women my age sat cross-legged on the sidewalk with their silver jewelry and key chains proudly displayed. I knew we didn't have much time, so I started buying as soon as the vendors appeared. I was excited to be a part of the commerce in a foreign land! I liked bartering in broken Spanish and purchasing handicrafts made in this exotic locale. By the time we reached the city, I had bought something from almost everyone who had asked.

I had never seen poverty and debauchery like this before. There were children in T-shirts and underwear selling boxes of mints, men advertising for live sex shows and offering us margaritas. Was I Pinocchio? Was this Pleasure Island? Among all the tourists and residents, I felt strangely anonymous. No one here looked like me, spoke like me, or knew anything about me and the way I was supposed to behave. I could buy anything I wanted, indulge in every desire I felt, and do it all under a cloak of invisibility.

Tijuana was fucking amazing! There was a donkey painted like a zebra; a donkey pulling carts of children; and a donkey advertised as having sex on stage. When I asked the man how that was possible, he took one look at us, let out a smug little chortle, and waved us past: "It's not for you." The only donkey show I'd ever known was one in which Mary rode the donkey into Bethlehem. The options here were endless. We could go anywhere, do anything, and experience it all! We wanted to go somewhere local, something quintessentially Mexican, so we decided on Señor Frog's.

At no point did anyone ever mention Katie waiting for us back in Newport Beach.

The leader of our group Stavros Skedros, a worldly Greek god who was only a junior but carried himself with enough swagger that he was on the senior trip. He was the one who had suggested the off-the-record excursion to Tijuana and had been the main motivator in my jumping ship from the good kids caravan. We followed him through the glass doors of Señor Frogs and waltzed up to the bar as if we had been doing it our entire lives. I was floating on air. We pretended to be world travelers: smooth, experienced, social, and wealthy. Stavros ordered me a piña colada and I came alive the second I popped the maraschino cherry into my mouth. A conga line erupted, and I joined in enthusiastically. At some point, a random patron placed a black felt cowboy hat on my head and it immediately became my entire personality. It's incredible what a little rum in the sun can do for the soul. I threw my head back and clasped the hat with one hand like a rodeo queen as I danced around the bar like a wild-winged dove on the edge of seventeen.

When Guillermo the burly bar hand came by offering shots, the crowd unanimously pointed him in my direction. He was a heavyset, heavily bronzed BBS—my favorite type: a big, buff shorty—but he possessed an added quality that transcended all his physical features. Guillermo, like me, was a showman. He knew how to work a crowd, with his holstered bottles of tequila and his plastic black whistle. I instantly became his willing muse. He began blowing his whistle in short blasts, in rhythm with the clapping crowd. He gallantly removed his glass bottle of unlabeled clear liquid from his leather belt along with a dingy fingerprint-stained shot glass, stretching his arm out to hold them together high up in one massive hand like Simba in *The Lion King*. The crowd roared.

I picked up on the energy and tipped my black hat toward my fans in appreciation. With his other arm, he grabbed me, spun me around, and held me tightly facing the crowd. I could feel his sweat and his belly pressed up against my back, and my body moved in time to his heavy breathing. He wrapped his arms around me and expertly poured the liquid into the cup as the throng cheered him on. He put the bottle back in its sheath and gave one final shrill of the whistle. I didn't have time to panic because, in that same instant, he thrust the glass between my lips and simultaneously grabbed my forehead, pressing it back to his chest, forcing the liquid down my throat. He then ceremoniously took a white cloth from his belt and pressed it to my lips to wipe off any spillage. It was all things sinister and greasy and dark and forced and exhilarating. I didn't care that it was two dollars a shot; I wanted more. It was cheap, but we were poor. I had just paid a street vendor two dollars for a set of silver bangles I planned to pass on to my future children and, while I knew alcoholism was also a trait you could pass on, it still felt indulgent.

We danced around in the mob of sweaty tourists and spent all the crumpled dollar bills we had scrounged from our parents' couch cushions and junk drawers. Guillermo made his rounds with his black whistle and holstered booze. I watched as he performed the shot-glass ritual with the other patrons. *Was it the same routine every time?* I wondered. *Was everyone clasped to his belly with such passion, such intent?* It didn't seem possible. What we had was special. Sure, he blew the whistle for customers young and old, male and female, wherever the money was flying, but there was no denying what I had felt in his grasp: the tequila on my tongue, the act foreign and forbidden, the fire burning in my heart. We had chemistry. I felt more alive than I ever had before. In that moment, I was infinite. There were no clocks, no parents, no rules, no friends waiting patiently on beaches.

By the time Guillermo circled back in my direction, his tequila bottles were half empty, just like my souvenir cash. I had no more dollar bills to wave in the air, and he had no reason to approach me. But we locked eyes across the bar. And in that instant, he let out a loud shrill of the whistle and began walking right toward me. My heart pounded with each whistle blurt, and before I could say, "Yes! *Pero no tengo dinero.* No parents, no rules, no boundaries, *NO MONEY!*" he grabbed my hand, spun me around, held me tight, and forced another shot down. The crowd approved and cheered. I leaned in through my drunken haze and did what came naturally: I grabbed his giant face and pulled him in for a kiss. Not a grandpa-greeting kiss, not even a meet-you-under-the-mistletoe kiss, but the kiss of a dying woman stranded in the desert thirsting for her last drop of water. It was the kiss of a girl who knew this was it: her only chance, her one moment to have a foreign love affair, to taste tequila on her lover's tongue. Once I walked back over the border, there would once again be expectations and standards and environments beyond my control. So this was, quite honestly, *it.*

Guillermo kissed back ... I think. As I attacked him with my mouth, the crowd went strangely quiet, and then luckily, after an awkward beat, began cheering reluctantly. They gave a confused reaction, as if considering, "Are we supposed to clap? We shouldn't be clapping for this . . ."

Mi amor was around thirty years old—it was hard to tell—with a weathered face and a handlebar mustache. He was definitely a Big Buff Shorty, emphasis on the big and the shorty of it all. He wore a thin white camp shirt that barely buttoned around his protruding belly, but it mattered not to me. I was enchanted. I finally pulled away and turned triumphantly to face my friends. Their horrified expressions were the first indication that I had misread the situation and that they were perhaps not supportive of my newfound relationship with Guillermo. Had they not felt our connection, our electricity? Had they not heard him blowing his whistle to the beat of my willing heart?

They had not. And their pained expressions confirmed it.

"You guys," I said, in an attempt to fill the awkward silence, "he never made me pay for that shot!" They didn't seem impressed. "I'm just saying, that's pretty awesome. I bet we could get more," I continued, hoping to lure them all into my seduction plan. Unfortunately, the sun was not only setting in Tijuana, but also on my hopeful future with the bar hand.

Teresa, who in light of recent events was now the most responsible one in our group, suggested that we start heading back. I had always pretended to be the responsible one, but this trip had taken an unexpected turn and the role had now deferred to Teresa. "We still need to pick up Katie," she reminded us.

"Katie . . . who is Katie?" Our earlier plans to return and meet her at the beach were a distant memory. I had completely forgotten about her! What time was it? We had told her we would be there by 2:00 p.m. at the latest, worst-case scenario. How much time had we wasted? We asked the hostess in broken Spanish if she had the time.

"*Seven p.m.*," she responded flatly in English.

Seven p.m.? We still had a thirty-minute walk to the car, then a two-hour drive back to Newport Beach, and we were already FIVE HOURS behind schedule.

"We need to hurry," I offered earnestly. Everyone nodded enthusiastically, as if hurrying at this point would help.

We had no idea what we were doing or where we were really going. There was a bank of Mexican pay phones along the walkway, but we had no money and no number to call. Our plan had simply been to return to the beach house to find Katie enjoying a few hours of sun in the sand. We didn't have a phone number for the beach house or even the actual address; when we left, we figured we would be able to find it just on sight. But now that it was dark and foreboding, we couldn't imagine how we had been so stupid.

We drove back quickly and began theorizing possible outcomes for Katie.

"I bet she decided to pile into someone else's car."

"There's no way she'll still be there."

If she had found a free spot in one of the caravan of vehicles, we wouldn't know until all the cars arrived safely in Salt Lake City, which was at least a thirteen-hour drive. We had no way of reaching the other drivers, and there was no way we were going to call our parents from a pay phone in Tijuana to see if anyone else had told them how Katie was going to get home. We were fucked.

We decided that it was probably best just to go by the beach house to make sure she wasn't there. We convinced ourselves she wouldn't be and that we'd continue on our own journey and all have a good laugh together when we saw Katie back at home.

By the time we got to Newport Beach, it was pitch black out, and all of the houses looked exactly the same. We couldn't distinguish between a pale blue three-story and a vanilla three-story. The butter yellow house looked strikingly familiar to the seafoam green one in the foggy street lighting.

Once it was clear that we couldn't be certain of the exact house, we decided to look for Katie on the beach. It was close to 10:00 p.m., and the beach was vacant. I saw a huddled mass in the darkness and ran up to it frantically, only to discover that it was just a firepit. The ocean breeze was blowing in off the water, and we decided as a group that it was much too cold and too dark for Katie to have stayed there. How stupid could she be?! She clearly had gone home in another car.

As we wandered along the boardwalk toward the parking lot, Teresa looked up in recognition. "Hey! I think this was our house," she called out. We walked up to the cement barrier bordering the patio and inspected the scene. There were lights on in the upstairs bedrooms, but there was no sign of life or light on the main floor, with the exception of a small kitchen lamp shining through the sliding glass doors.

Stavros was the first to notice.

"There's a note on the door," he said, as he climbed over the barrier. He walked up and pulled a two-by-two-inch yellow square Post-it note off the plate glass. He brought it back to us on the beach. The words were scrawled in blue ballpoint pen, and we had to hold it up under the streetlight to read it: "If you're looking for Katie, she is at 14566 Placentia Ave."

We all began screaming and cheering triumphantly. "Oh my gosh! We found her! We did it! We're heroes!" We reveled in our joy and congratulated each other on our tenacity and problem solving. A fun caper and case well-solved. Our joy doubled when we realized that we were *on* Placentia Ave. and we would only have to walk a few houses away to pick her up.

We were laughing and talking and celebrating our happy ending when we knocked on the door of 14566 Placentia Ave. A gentle gray-haired woman answered, with an expression of relief and frustration.

"Hi! Is our friend Katie here?" we asked as if it were the most natural thing in the world. Like a set of new parents picking their toddler up from daycare.

She met our smiles with a disappointed frown and opened the door wider to reveal a huddled figure slowly approaching from the hallway. It might have been Katie, but she was barely recognizable. Her face was swollen to twice its size and was smeared with ointment covering her charred brick-red skin with a crackling glaze. Her lips were swollen and hung open, trout-like, covered in oozing yellow blisters. A hush fell over the group and we stood there, staring at what we had done. On instinct, I somberly removed the black felt hat from my head and held it reverently against my chest, my eyes cast down in respect for the walking dead.

"WHAT HAPPENED?" someone finally gasped. Katie opened her mouth to speak, but before a sound could come out, she grimaced in pain.

"She's sunburnt," the lady said without emotion. "You left her out there all day."

"Oh no! Did you forget to put on sunscreen?"

Her rescuer answered for her: "No, she didn't have sunscreen. She

67

didn't have water, and she didn't have food. I noticed her earlier in the day with all of her luggage camped out on the beach and asked her if she needed help. She refused and said that her friends would be by any minute. She didn't want to move away from your meeting spot because she was afraid she would miss you. When it got dark and cold, I went out again and convinced her to leave a note at the house you rented and wait here with me."

The cloud of shame was so thick that we could barely choke out a few apologetic thank-yous as we shuffled Katie, now shivering with aftershocks, to the car.

The first few hours of the drive back home were mostly silent. We took turns driving in shifts and exchanging guilty glances while Katie slept, mouth ajar, in the back seat. It was well past midnight when we hit the freeway, and we still had a good twelve hours to go. We were fueled by shame and regret and fear of getting caught now that Katie was a clear casualty. No one felt like listening to music, Garth Brooks or otherwise, and we were afraid to talk about our adventures for fear that Katie would wake up and overhear, and we'd be exposed as the selfish time-blind assholes that we were.

When the sun finally rose, it illuminated the interior of the car enough for us to examine the damage to Katie's cracked face and hands closely. Crusts had begun to form in some of the cracks in her skin, and new blisters were forming spontaneously on her forehead and cheeks, leaving a trail of tiny amber-colored liquid that looked like something out of a medieval spell book. Her eyes were swollen to tiny slits and it was hard to tell if she was awake or sleeping. When she finally woke up, the rage and disappointment fueled her with enough strength to speak and tell us what she had been through.

Apparently, back at the beach house, checkout time had been strictly enforced. It was close to noon, and everyone had managed to get up, pack up, clean up, and load up their cars in time, despite my doubtful prediction. Katie was the only straggler, sitting on the boardwalk on the other side of the cement barrier as the property managers prepared for their next guests. No one wanted to leave Katie alone on the beach, but she reassured them that we had a plan. We were going to be back any minute and would pick her up and drive home to Utah together. We hadn't factored her luggage into her lounging on the beach, biding time until we returned, so she'd lugged roller bags a few feet onto the sand and set up camp, counting the minutes until we showed up. Meanwhile, in Mexico, we were not counting the minutes, but rather the number of shots of tequila we could afford from Guillermo. No one could ever know.

Even though Katie was furious with us, she still took one for the team, concealing our escapades when we got home by claiming that she'd simply underestimated the strength of the California sun. It took days before she talked to any of us again; weeks before my guilt subsided; and months before I made back the hole I'd burned in my wallet.

Señor Frog's was the first time I had given the Good-Time Girl permission to live without inhibition. If I had been self-aware enough to recognize how much I loved everything about that little exploit, I would've done it a lot more! But there had been consequences, real and imagined, that seemed to confirm what I'd always been taught: wickedness never was happiness. Even the smallest sins have eternal consequences. Katie's sunburnt face and hands were a reminder of how hot Hell's fires burn for sinners, and I felt devastated that she paid the price for my folly. I had done something bad and people had gotten hurt. There was no such thing as harmless fun.

I knew I wasn't going to move to Mexico to marry a bartender, but there was a part of me that wanted to . . . and I wish I had been brave enough to ask myself why. Living a life outside of what I had imagined was out of the realm of possibility, no matter how alluring it seemed. I would never have forgiven myself if I had sold my birthright for a black plastic whistle and a felt sombrero south of the border. But I was eighteen, and that was what I wanted. And I felt bad because of it.

I hid the photos we took in Tijuana and prayed that no one would ever find them. I opened my mouth no wider than Katie's sunburnt lips to tell the tale and kept the secret for years. I still needed to go to BYU, and if they found out I had been drinking, they could revoke my acceptance. If I told anyone about Señor Frog's, it would put my whole future at risk. I chalked it up as a wrinkle in time, an illicit experience to store away for the dark, cold winter of life as a teetotaler.

But every day there is less of a need to hide. With a little perspective, what once was a character-defining failure has now become a funny anecdote. Despite that growth, this is the first time I'm publicly telling the story. And when I say it out loud, I have to remind myself: "Heather, just say you went to *Mexico*. You don't have to say the city. I know you loved it, but Tijuana isn't cool."

SEVEN

MS. MARTHA BOURNE

My first job after graduating from high school was as an assistant tech writer at the company where my older sister Jenny was the front desk receptionist. She got me the job and was my guide and mentor throughout the whole process, giving me inside information on the company executives, the break room, the best places to have lunch nearby, and the employees I should try to avoid. When she found out that I'd be sharing an office space with Martha Bourne, she squealed.

"She's my favorite person here. She is so funny. You are going to love her. She's in her twenties, from North Carolina, and she plays the piano. Also . . . she's a writer!"

A writer, I thought, *just like me.*

I was not a writer, unless you considered my stab at the My America speech contest a work of literature. But this job had "assistant writing tasks" in its description, so I was eager to try it on for size. And it surprised me how much I liked it. A fellow writer. Someone I could look up to and emulate. I immediately thought of a blonde, busty super-model like Kate Upton, only I pictured her with brown hair, because she was in academia after all. She was clearly a college graduate, so I assumed she had been president of the best sorority on campus. I could live vicariously through her experiences as a Delta Gamma, and politely explain to her why I had decided to attend a university where fraternities and sororities were forbidden. "It sounds really fun, Martha, but we don't have mimosa brunches at BYU. We have something we like to call 'honor' instead."

The fact that Martha was from North Carolina told me all I needed to know about her faith. She wasn't from Utah, so she probably wasn't a Mormon. This was going to be a missionary opportunity. I had been taught that as a member of the Church of Jesus Christ of Latter Day Saints, it was my duty (and privilege) to represent the church every time I met someone new. My sister was a righteous rule-abiding Mormon, and I was sure everyone at the office expected no less from me. I would never be able to reveal my escapades in Tijuana or my private secret doubts to someone outside the faith, especially if they were looking to me as an example of just how great the church was. You can count on me, Jesus! I was going to show her just how cool, evolved, and ultimately right Mormons were. And I was the perfect girl to do it. After all, I was a "cool" Mormon. I could make out with a bartender in Tijuana *and* teach a Sunday School lesson. I could hang with the big dogs—a woman of the world like Martha—without losing my testimony. I couldn't wait to impress her. I needed to repent for my recent hijinks on my senior trip and preaching the gospel to Martha would give me the perfect opportunity. I would never sully the church's reputation or admit to her that I had tried tequila. I couldn't even admit it to myself. I would lead with perfection and protocols from here on out.

This was nothing new for me. Whenever I met someone new, I found myself caught between two worlds. My natural fun-loving self and the traditions I was brought up in—always choosing to leave my real identity behind and lead with the idealized version. I wasn't just representing the Church, I was representing the perfect person I hoped that I could become. I needed to be the happiest, most self-assured, committed righteous member even if I didn't feel it on the inside. And because being Mormon was the most central part of my identity, I always led with it. Once I convinced people that the Gospel really was the only way to be happy, then I could let down my guard a little bit and talk more openly. But it was duty to God first before duty to my true feelings.

There are a few nominal sins that you can commit when you are a member of the church where you can step off the beaten path and return innocuously: drinking, heavy petting, an illicit embrace with a bar hand. But there were bigger, more colossal cliffs that, if you stepped off of them, returning was not so easy: sex, homosexuality, teen pregnancy, abortion, divorce. I knew the house I wanted to live in, and I believed that I could only live in that house if I followed the teachings of the church. Whenever I was tempted to take field trips and see how the other half lived, they had to be temporary visits and nothing more.

I wanted to be seen as cool, but I also wanted to be known as virtuous. I envisioned Martha and me swapping stories about boys where I would gently encourage her to stop putting out because, "Why buy the cow when you can get the milk for free?" I had heard this said my entire life, and it made perfect sense. No one would be milking me unless they owned at least four acres and a farmhouse. I concocted pretend scenarios where I would show Martha how fun life could be if you lived the Gospel. I would show her how good boyfriends respected the women in their lives, which is why they kept their hands to themselves and their tongues in their mouth. I would explain, with reverence, that the more a man restrained himself, the more you knew he valued you. I had no actual experience with any of these things, but pretending to comforted me and gave me confidence. I, as Jesus's sunbeam, was going to shine so bright that I would burn her corneas.

When Virlene, my manager at Wasatch Education Systems, walked me on my very first day to the office space I'd be sharing with Martha, I saw her through the office glass and immediately thought there had been a mix-up. She was not the sorority girl I had anticipated.

I had put hot rollers in my hair that morning and selected a bright floral romper from The Limited for our first meeting, but it appeared that Martha had done no outfit planning whatsoever. She was wearing what can be best described as a men's bowling shirt, black Doc Marten boots, and shorts that were *kind of* like pants but definitely not identifiable as pedal pushers or clam diggers.

I had never seen anyone like her. She wore no makeup or jewelry aside from a few cloth bracelets/leftover concert wristbands and a black rubber band on her wrist. It looked like she even had a chain on her wallet. If I half-closed my eyes, she looked a lot like a mashup of Amy Ray from the Indigo Girls and a young k.d. lang. If those two women morphed into one bad-ass rocker, they might look exactly like Martha Bourne. She was nothing like the all-American writer clutching a copy of *Wuthering Heights* that I'd envisioned.

I immediately told myself that she was not my type of girl. Everything about her threatened what I thought I was supposed to be and it made me uncomfortable. I was eighteen, but I thought I needed to be unwavering in my convictions. How could I embrace a friendship with someone so obviously different than me? I thought of how much I loved the Indigo Girls and figured that if I had found space in my heart for their music, I could also make room for Martha. I gave myself permission to transfer all of my unfettered affection for them onto her and hoped for the best.

She's Jenny's favorite person? I thought. This surprised me to my core. *My sister must have a wild side I don't know about.* This was my first professional environment, and Martha did not look professional. These were the days of nylons and pencil skirts. Casual Fridays did not exist, and Martha was Casual Friday seven days a week. Her dark brown hair was cut short and blunt just below her chin, and she ran both hands through it at the same time when she was frustrated. I mean that act alone proved how different we were. Did she have any idea how the oils from your hands transferred directly to the shaft of your cuticle? Her voice was gravelly and serious. My dreams of swapping hot-girl secrets and her giving me hand-me-down makeup samples popped like a cartoon bubble above my head. Martha was not going to be buying me my first Chanel bag as a going-away present when I started at BYU in the fall.

Martha immediately skipped any and all niceties and small talk. As soon as I walked into the office, she slid her roller chair back and sized me up. I assumed she would immediately dismiss me.

But she didn't. Instead, she broke off a piece of her shoelace and taped it up to her upper lip like a mustache, adopting a new persona named *Monsieur Marceau*. I did not think I would be able to goof off in a corporate setting, but with Martha that's practically all we did. Suddenly, being professional was the last thing I cared about. Just like my sister had predicted, she quickly became my favorite person. I was totally drawn in.

Our office was in the main hallway and had floor-to-ceiling windows that showcased us to anyone passing by. Our desks were arranged so that we sat facing opposite walls with our backs to each other. In order to chat, we'd have to swivel around in our office chairs, making it glaringly obvious to every one in the building that we weren't hard at work. I was reprimanded more than once by my supervisors, but I didn't care. I wanted to do a good job, but I wanted to talk to Martha more.

I wanted to talk to her about everything. I pestered her nonstop with my saintly bullshit, constantly spouting my theories on life and eternity, convincing her how happy I was in a platonic relationship with a boy who had designed our dream home, shaved his entire body daily, and had promised marriage even though he said it was a sin to kiss while you're both lying down. Martha would roll her eyes and look at me like I was crazy.

"Don't set a goal to just be a wife," she would encourage. "Set a goal to be something to yourself."

When I tried to brag about other hypothetical crushes on boys, she wouldn't pretend she cared: "Don't date that bozo. He's not the one for you. Whether or not he likes you is irrelevant. You don't like him. Stop pretending that you do."

I knew she was right, but I couldn't admit it. She was the smartest, coolest person I had ever met, and she saw right through me.

She was a rock star. And I mean that literally. I soon discovered that Martha Bourne was the lead singer in a band called My Sister Jane. I was underage, but she put my name on the list for all their shows in Salt Lake City, and smuggled me in for my first backstage experiences. I'd follow the Janes for a set at the Dead Goat Saloon and other venues in downtown Salt Lake. It was the first time I'd ever been in bars like that and it felt slightly criminal. Her fans went crazy whenever they performed, and I felt myself torn with admiration and jealousy, but also judgment.

Sure, they were having a good time *now*, but it wouldn't last. It couldn't last. Everything I believed told me that no matter how enticing their bohemian lifestyle looked, it ultimately couldn't make them happy. Not eternally happy in the way that mattered. True happiness came in a very specific package: a pure wife, a providing husband, and a very specific, gendered wardrobe that did not include chains on wallets.

I was never sure that Martha was gay until she began mentioning her partner, Julie. I had never met a real lesbian before. I was cautious but curious. *You're a lesbian? Cool. Cool. Cool. Cool.*

Martha invited me to the home she shared with her girlfriend and showed me how to dip chunks of French bread in olive oil and salt. When I first got the invite, I wasn't sure I should even go. But then once I was inside her house, I couldn't believe how normal it was. And homey. And seemingly sin free. She made her own hummus—her own goddamn hummus in a blender!—and she made it look so easy. I thought only stay-at-home moms made things from scratch, and I only understood cooking in terms of feeding a family. I didn't know it was something lesbians could do for fun. But Martha's house had adult furniture and a dining table with a full set of china. I thought china was something you only got when you were married and had registered for it. Why did she care about being such a homemaker if she was a rock star and also . . . a lesbian? If you were a lesbian, wasn't it because you hated all the things that women had to do for the men in their lives? These revelations I had about Martha revealed how narrow my expectations were for my own ambition. I didn't know that, as women, we were allowed to be many things at one time, and that figuring all of it out was just part of the process.

When I went into the kitchen, I noticed a Polaroid taped to her fridge. I walked over and looked at it closely. I was immediately embarrassed. It was a candid pic of Martha's girlfriend wearing men's white underwear. I felt like I had stumbled on something dirty that I wasn't supposed to see. This was exactly why I didn't have friends that I didn't go to church with! I glanced around hoping no one had seen me look at the pic, but Martha was already walking over.

"Isn't that great?" she asked. I pretended to be confused about what she was referring to. She reached over and pulled the pic off the fridge. "I took this! She looks so fucking sexy. Don't you think?" My cheeks flushed with embarrassment. How was I supposed to know? Even if I did think she looked sexy, I would never have admitted it. I wasn't afraid of sliding around on the Kinsey Scale, but I was afraid to make the connection between deviance and sexiness in case I ignited a dark force that would somehow haunt me forever. And a woman wearing men's underpants seemed to me at the time to be walking the razor's edge of kink.

Martha was unfazed by my stammering and moved on. She buzzed around the house setting up plates and wine and flowers. Nothing about her outward appearance screamed hostess and homemaker, but here she was being a great hostess and homemaker. If only she'd invest in a push-up bra and some red bottom shoes, we could be twin flames. But where I was just an ember, I knew Martha was a bonfire. If I got too close or embraced her lifestyle too much, I'd end up getting burned.

Instead, I talked to her about marriage. I waxed philosophical about how there was nothing more noble than laying down your own life and ambitions for a man you loved and for the opportunity to create a family with him. I knew what I was saying sounded self-righteous and preachy, but that was on purpose. The more frequently and the louder that I said it, the more I hoped I'd believe it. I was a Mormon goddammit. And this was life as it had been laid out for me—grander and greater than any romantic dream. Love/passion/ambition had nothing to do with it. I was a breeder; pedigrees and purpose were the only things that mattered. I was learning to be a true hypocrite. When I saw Martha living a lifestyle that I found tempting, I judged her the harshest.

I was in full projection mode. My antics in Tijuana had rattled me, so I shouted from the rooftops just how much I wanted to be good in order to compensate for how much fun I had being bad. Looking back on the way I acted and the things I said, I'm astonished that Martha didn't spend two days with me, march me out to the sidewalk, and give me a good curb stomp with her Doc Marten boot. I would have deserved it. But she somehow managed to be my friend without judging me, and I failed to follow that same example.

I loved her, but I judged her. And it never occurred to me that she just let me get away with it. She protected my naiveté in ways that I didn't understand until much later in life.

If I had been able to be honest with myself back then, what I really wanted was to be exactly like her, to be immersed in her world. Martha represented radical acceptance and complete independence. Thirty years ago, she was living in a way that I still dream about today.

"Yo, Ma! Start living your life, girl! You're allowed to want more. You *are* more, and you've always known it. Now go do it."

Martha was the first person I truly admired who wasn't Mormon. I could've said, "Martha, I don't want to go to BYU and get married and have kids right away. I want to live a different kind of life." And she would've helped me. She would've guided me. She would've told me it was okay: "Hells yeah, you do! I'm glad you finally came to your senses. Now dump that preachy attitude and start being real." She was the first adult in my life that would have given me permission to leave the church. But instead, I felt that pull and I squashed it. I reminded myself of all the reasons I didn't want to leave, of all the reasons I didn't want to swim upstream and be disruptive. I retreated into the cavern of the world that had been planned for me, and I pretended to be thrilled about it.

No matter how much I wanted to fit in with Martha and her friends, I knew their life could never be mine; it wasn't an option. I was pretty sure I wasn't a lesbian, but it wouldn't have mattered even if I was. I was willing to sacrifice being seen, being understood, and being valued for the mystery prize of the new and everlasting covenant that Mormonism promised me waiting behind curtain-door number three. And I didn't want to be constantly reminded of the freedom and independence that Martha enjoyed. I didn't want to question my choices or to think too hard about who I was and what I was giving up, so I pulled away. My job was over at the end of the summer, and I assumed that meant that my friendship with Martha was as well. We started calling each other less and less. I stopped showing up at her shows and showing any reciprocity, and my friendship with Martha Bourne and all her gloriousness faded into oblivion.

But the memory of Martha has never left me. I wasn't prepared for someone who lived so differently to be able to see me so clearly, and it challenged everything I knew about myself and my future. I was supposed to shun Martha's way of life, but instead I felt inexplicably drawn to her. And what I couldn't express in words, Tom Waits expressed best in song: "Martha. Martha, I love you, can't you see?" I loved Martha for all the unlived dreams she was living on my behalf. I loved Martha for seeing beyond my facade. I loved Martha for changing the world and blazing her own trail. And I love Martha still because she expanded my expectations of what it means to be a woman, and what it means to be a friend.

I recently reconnected with Martha and told her I was writing about her in my book. She's an adjunct professor at the Berklee College of Music in Boston and writes musical scores for movies and more. When we talked, it was like no time had passed at all. She told me to stop getting plastic surgery and to go see *Hadestown* on Broadway. We made promises to meet, and I threatened to show up at one of her classes on campus to make a scene and prove to her that people everywhere in every industry watch *The Real Housewives*, even if she doesn't.

EIGHT

CINNAMON GIRL

Before I went off to college, I'd seen all the college-themed movies: *Animal House, Back to School, Revenge of the Nerds* . . . I spoke the language of student affairs with fluency, and I believed myself to be prepared for all that four years of undergrad had in store for someone like me—an impressionable young blonde willing to do a lot for a little. But BYU was anything but fruitful in pursuit of anything but academic rigor and marital engagements. You went to BYU to get your MRS. degree, not to have a good time. I had to get rid of all my Hollywood dreams of a collegiate romance on the frat-house floor or a sordid tryst in a quiet aisle of the library. I would have loved to have had an illicit affair with an aging professor, but that was never going to happen. The closest I ever got was Alan Smithson.

At BYU, I never called my professors by their first name. It was always Professor, Dr., Mr., Bishop, or even more creepy, "Brother." Alan went by Alan, not Professor Smithson because he was not one. He was a technical writing instructor. To call him Professor Smithson would have been to commit fraud. And yet, he refused to allow us to call him Mr. Smithson because he felt that his relationship to us did not require such a formal title. It was clear that he considered himself one of us: a glorified student; an inspiration first, friend second; and an actual teacher only when forced.

On the first day of class, he wandered up and down the aisles telling us about his off-season adventures as a volunteer reserve fireman, explaining how he wasn't going to let the fact that he was thirty-one and unmarried keep him from embracing a full life. He was wiry and blond and was flouting BYU grooming standards by wearing his straight hair deceptively long in a modified bowl cut. He looked like Little Lord Fauntleroy with a giant bald spot. His skin was pale and didn't appear to be weathered like you'd imagine a wilderness fireman's to be. He wore little round eyeglasses that occasionally fogged up when he got really excited, and he had a chain attached from the wallet in his back pocket to the belt loop of his khakis, a la Martha Bourne. It might have been this tiny detail that ignited my heart. He was the most brazen rebel I had seen employed at BYU, and I immediately fell in love with him.

I didn't want to come on too strong, but I was pretty sure he was feeling what I was feeling. How could he not? We were connected. He was a salmon swimming upstream like I wanted to be, rebuffing the cultural pressures of the church to marry, settle down, and have a responsible career. He was lost. Wandering. Looking for the missing puzzle piece to complete him. *Fear not, Alan Smithson, for I am here.* I could be his new North Star.

Alan existed at a unique intersection that allowed me to live the Hollywood movie fantasy while still remaining within the bounds of my hopeful, church-filled future. I wanted to fall in love with a professor the way I'd seen it happen on screen, but if I did, he'd have to marry me. Alan was young enough and his resumé just lackluster enough to make him attainable. Now that I was his student, I could cross two things off my bucket list in one fell swoop: (1) have a love affair with a "professor" and (2) still get married in the temple. Once he deflowered me, he would own me, and we would build a life together teaching freshman-level GE courses and fighting fires when the real firemen were tapped out and needed to call in the reserves.

Alan was adrift from the pack. He was not imbued with the same arrogance and infallibility of every guy I had met so far on campus. At BYU, every eligible nineteen- to twenty-one-year-old male is not on campus; he is out in the world serving an LDS mission. Every man I met was twenty-one or older and was a returned missionary looking for a wife as admonished by the leaders of the church. But despite BYU being a breeding ground for potential partners, I still remained single. Alan however, was different. This man had been beaten down by life; he had seen what was out there. He was thirty-one: past his prime, with a circular dome emerging like a tractor beam from the top of his head. He had been left behind by the competition, and he appeared to be exhibiting my favorite feature in a man: desperation. He needed me! I was settling for him, but that didn't matter in the grand scheme of things—what we lacked as individuals, we would make up for as a couple.

My entire college schedule quickly became centered around ENGL311 and my budding crush on Alan. I never missed a day of class. I curled my hair, applied multiple coats of mascara, and made sure I was sending out the "TAKE ME; I'M YOURS" signal as strong as the pungent scent of my Victoria's Secret Japanese Blossom body spray. I no longer alternated days that I washed my hair or wore sweats to class. Every day presented an opportunity to shoot my shot at the Prince, and Cinderella had to be ready for this ball. I absorbed every tiny detail he shared with us about his life: his favorite bands, his favorite restaurants, his favorite books. If he liked it, I liked it, even if I had no idea what he was referring to. Luckily for me, the classroom was his stage, and it was clear that he loved spending his lecture time sharing personal anecdotes for our approval.

In every class, he'd give us little writing assignments. One week, he asked us to describe a moment that had changed our lives. He started the lecture by telling us about the moment that had changed his: the death of his girlfriend. His tale was a sad one. As sad as any after-school special I had ever seen. And so well told that I doubted its veracity. But I didn't care if he was lying, as long as he was describing the type of girl he wanted to love.

He described meeting his dream girl in line at the grocery store. She was a sweet girl who not only shared his affinity for ten items or less in the express lane, but also for Neil Young and nature. She was a girl he wanted to take camping, take to movies, and take to concerts in outdoor amphitheaters. She was perfect. She completed his sentences and unfinished LEGO projects. He called her his Cinnamon Girl, and was planning a romantic proposal at sunset at Utah Lake when he got the call that she had been killed, taken far too soon in a fatal car accident. He wasn't sure he would ever recover. The classroom fell silent, and everyone sat surrounded by the tragedy of it all.

I immediately went home and put the song on repeat. I heard, *I wanna live with a Cinnamon Girl. I could be happy for the rest of my life with a Cinnamon Girl*, and cried my eyes out, vowing to heal his broken heart. A few weeks later, he gave the class an assignment to write about our favorite song. I chose "Cinnamon Girl" by Neil Young and didn't even feel like I was lying. It wasn't my favorite song before, but it was my favorite song now. Especially if it described the girl that Alan Smithson wanted me to be.

Based on the lyrics, it wasn't going to very difficult to be what Alan Smithson needed. According to the lyrics, a Cinnamon Girl was a dreamer of pictures and a chaser of moonlight. She was a girl that waited between shows, and ran in the night. I could do that! I could do ALL OF THAT! It would be a little difficult to demonstrate those qualities in the classroom, but I would find a way.

Admittedly, it would have been a lot more work for me if he had been a fan of Billy Joel. Then I would have had to be not only an Uptown Girl, but also More Than A Woman, and that required a lot. But this would be easy. I could Single White Female this Cinnamon Girl faster than he could imagine, and he would fall immediately in love with me.

When I went to class the following Tuesday, I felt transformed. I tried to communicate through my eyes that Neil Young had infiltrated every cell of my body and pulsed that energy towards him with a steady homing beat, but he didn't seem to notice. I would have done better to have written "I love you" on my eyelids, but I was seducing him the way I wanted to be seduced. By someone studying and analyzing the lyrics of a song that I referenced one time in one lecture. That's the type of love I longed for. And with my Cinnamon Girl essay, I was just getting started. I applied this technique to every lesson we had. When he asked us to write about natural phenomena, I wrote about wilderness fires that I spent hours researching and studying. When the assignment was to describe our perfect partner, I casually listed my ideal as men who were blond, balding, and five foot nine. I hoped he would read between the lines of every paper I turned in. Between every ellipsis, the message was clear: "Let your troubled heart be healed. I'm the one you've been looking for."

I turned my papers in and waited with anticipation for his scrawled analysis at the top of each page. Every word he wrote, I considered to be a love letter directed at me. I'd hoped that he recognized the same soulmate compatibility in me that I recognized in him. In each weekly writing assignment, I had to show him that I was smart and funny and campy and into nature. I wanted to prove that I was the answer to his prayers with every sentence I wrote.

When he announced his office hours for student interviews, my heart skipped a beat. I knew that this was the moment! It would be just me and him. No audience to observe; no fellow students to interfere. Just a small closet of an office-like space adjacent to his temporary classroom.

I prepared for our meeting like I was preparing for the prom, leaving behind me a chemtrail cloud of Japanese Blossom and cheap hair spray. When I approached, the door to his office was slightly open, and he welcomed me in, shuffling his papers and trying to tidy up, but it was clear that he had not been anticipating my arrival. He snuck a glance at the sign-up sheet to confirm who I was, and my heart fell.

"So, what brings you in here today . . ."

As if he didn't know I was there to consummate our relationship. Wasn't it obvious? We were in love! Hadn't he been writing "keep up the good work" on my papers for the last six weeks? Hadn't he been reading my innermost thoughts and pledges of love and affection? Had he not seen my essay where I had said Neil Young was my favorite artist and "Cinnamon Girl" my favorite song?

He was obviously playing it cool.

I wedged myself into the small chair with the desk attached and pulled out a file folder of papers that I pretended to want to go over. "I just want you to know how much I'm enjoying class," I said. "I just feel like I'm learning so much more in this class than any of my others . . ."

As soon as I flattered him, he took interest: "Oh really?" He pulled out his chair and collapsed into it, draping his leg sideways casually across the armrest.

Suddenly, I felt like I was in over my head. The movies hadn't told me what to do next. They made it seem so easy: a young, able-bodied, willing girl goes into the professor's office, throws down a few pithy seduction lines, and the rest just happens naturally. And yet, somehow, this process seemed to be requiring much more effort. I had already overhauled my entire personality and curated my personal catalog of favorite musicians and songs and clothing to meet this man's seemingly simple requirements and still nothing was happening.

"Yeah, we've got a pretty good class," he said. "I'm glad you're getting a lot out of it."

An awkward pause.

"What's your major?" he asked, almost as if he was obligated.

"I'm majoring in humanities," I replied. "Mostly because what I really want to do is be a mother." This was the line that you always said after you declared your major in order to assure whoever you were talking to that you had no ambitions outside of loving and keeping a home. You could brag all you wanted about your grades and your accomplishments so long as every road led to enriching your ability as a wife and mother. I had the playbook memorized, so it was easy for me to stay on script.

"Have you ever thought about what you might want to do if you don't get married?" he asked, almost like a dare. I internally recoiled.

How brazen of him! Nobody dared to ask a girl at BYU that question . . . that was like asking if you were afraid to get hit by a bus every time you left your house. It's not that it's an offensive question. It just posed a violent potential reality that we chose to block out of our minds. Of course, we knew that unmarried life existed somewhere out there in the ether, but we didn't like to think about it, and we definitely didn't like to think that it would ever befall us or anyone we knew.

I wasn't in Alan's office asking him to marry me. I wasn't even in his office asking him to sleep with me; I hadn't thought that far ahead. I'd assumed that all I needed to do was get him alone and in private for him to then take the lead. I thought I was putting a piece of bread in front of a starving man, and once I gave him the signal, his primal instinct would take over. But this guy didn't even know my name. To him, I was just one of thirty other technical writing students. I had been dedicating every paper, note, question, and comment in his class in order to express my desire for him, and he was absolutely oblivious.

This was not a meet-cute for me and Alan Smithson; this was just a Tuesday. I was writing him essays; I was booking his office hours; I was laughing at his jokes. I was his goddamn Cinnamon Girl. But the subtleties were clearly getting me nowhere. So I leaned in: "Do you ever date your students?"—almost trembling as I got the words out. How much more could I lay it down in front of this guy?

He took the bait, but not in the way that I wanted him to. His eyes twinkled, and I watched the split-second play out on his face as we transitioned from student–teacher to ally–friend. My heartbeat quickened.

"You know, of course there've been opportunities," he bragged. "But I'm pretty selective." A sneaky grin spread across his face. This was it. What I had seen in the movies. This was why I had spent two and a half hours primping for a twenty-minute open-call slot during office hours. He leaned forward in his chair and said, "There's actually a girl in our class that is totally my type."

Wait . . . WHAT?! A smile exploded on my face. I couldn't help it. My faith in myself was immediately restored. I hadn't gotten it wrong; he was just being being coy. I simply had to overcome all the social barriers prohibiting him from declaring his love, and now it was happening just as I had imagined. I had lobbed the softball, and he was hitting it out of the park. This was it; this was the moment!

"Oh really?" I cooed.

"Yeah," he said with a smile.

I smiled back.

"Her name is Stephanie."

. . .

Stephanie?!?

I was speechless. He leaned back in his chair, interlocked his fingers, and put his hands behind his head, letting out a dreamy sigh.

"Yeah, man. She drives me crazy. It's so funny that you asked me that. Was it that obvious?" he asked. "She's basically my dream girl. You know, real tiny, petite. Brunette."

The walls were caving in on me. What the fuck did he just say? *Stephanie?* I knew exactly who Stephanie was and sorry to say it buddy but she's way out of your league. She was gorgeous and stylish and so thin her shoulder blades jutted out like little wings. She didn't even use a backpack, she just sauntered into class carrying her notebook casually, and she always needed to borrow a pen. She wore three stackable gold bangles on her left wrist that would've clanged together if she had ever raised her hand, but luckily she never did. I had never heard her ask a question, or comment in a discussion, or even laugh when he made his dumb dad jokes. *Fucking Stephanie? She may be your type, but have you looked in the mirror? You are not hers.*

The idea of him being with a girl like Stephanie made the dismissal feel more manageable. *Okay. Okay. So you have your dream girl. Ask her out, get rejected, and I'll be your rebound. The girl that sticks around to pick up all the pieces once they fall apart.*

Hope was not lost: "So, what are you going to do?" I asked. "Are you going to ask her out?"

I transitioned quickly to the friend role. Even in the face of clear and final rejection, I still wasn't going to give up. Maybe this was the point in our relationship where we talked about our ideals and then circled back to discussing why we would end up settling for each other.

I assumed he would say, "No, no. I'd never dare. That's why I'm here with you telling you how I feel about her. She's nothing more than a pipe dream."

But that's not how it went.

"Yeah. We've gone out a couple of times," he said. "But she feels weird about it because of the whole teacher–student thing. So we're probably going to cool it off until after the semester."

They had gone out a few times? On purpose? Like she had actually agreed to a date? That meant she actually liked him. And if she liked *him*, what did that mean for *me*? I had gone after Alan because he was already shelved in the dented and scratched bin. He was a bargain basement love option that I hoped would feel forever indebted. This wasn't just rejection. This was a shift in the way I saw myself and, more importantly, how I realized men, even the desperate ones, saw me.

I suddenly understood that he didn't need someone to study his favorite songs, study his career history, study his passions. He didn't need a girl to labor over every word in every essay, and hang on every word in every lecture. He was perfectly capable of seeing what he wanted, going after it, and getting it.

Everything I had written, everything I had done, everything I had dreamed about was in vain. I had wasted the entire semester pining after a man that didn't even know I existed. I was not a piece of bread in front of a starving man, I wasn't even on the menu. This guy wasn't even walking into my restaurant. It didn't matter what music I liked, what I wrote, what made me interesting . . . and it never would.

The entire world I had created existed only to me. Alan didn't know or realize that I wanted him because he didn't know or realize that I was even there. I was just invisible: too big, too blond, too fucking earnest. Whatever the reasons were, I wasn't registering. I had tried to sparkle, to shine, to show him my personality quirks that would blend so effortlessly with his, but I never considered whether he noticed any of it. I had given him papers that I had written not for class, but for him—to impress him, to woo him, to lure him out of his preconceived notions of who I was and why I didn't matter, and to convince him that I was someone who could be his Cinnamon Girl.

But I never would be. And I wanted to make sure that I felt this rejection fully. I didn't want to think back on this moment and gaslight myself into thinking it had happened differently. I didn't want to lie to myself and pretend that there still might've been a chance.

"I had no idea that was your type," I said.

"Oh yeah," he said. "You know, just kind of quiet."

With a strong mix of desperation and resignation, I revealed myself. "I kind of hoped I would be your type . . ."

He seemed taken aback—amused, but definitely not interested.

"Really?" he asked.

"Really," I said. "I thought you were going to be my one affair with a professor."

It felt good to just say it out loud—to acknowledge my delusion; to acknowledge that I was way out in left field; to acknowledge that the dream was so far gone, the reverie so broken, it had paved the way for only abject humility. How was he going to react now that I had ripped my beating heart out and placed it right on his paper-strewn, shitty metal desk that he shared with two other student instructors?

"What if I just took you right now and had my way with you?" he mused.

I wanted to laugh, but I was processing what he had said. *Please, oh please. Take me. That's all I've ever wanted.*

I wanted to say what I was thinking: "I'd fuck your brains out," but I was a virgin, and I had no idea how to fuck someone regularly, let alone fuck their brains out. Besides, saying that, regardless of what had prompted it, would have definitely gotten me a quick visit to the Honor Code Office. And that most likely would have gotten me expelled from his class, and from the school—tuition not reimbursed. And whether or not I got my brains fucked out by my student instructor wouldn't even matter if I had to say it out loud to *him*. How desperate.

"I don't know. I don't know what I'd do," I stammered.

He grinned and reclined farther in his seat. Relishing the one-sided adoration that hung in the air. The defeat swallowed me whole. I tried to make a joke and laugh it all off as fun banter between two Neil

Young–loving fools. "Hahaha. Well, I guess we'll never know." I looked for his reaction. Was he laughing? Was he crying? Did he at least like me as a friend? As a student?

At the end of the semester, Alan Smithson gave me a fucking A-minus in the class. Not even a solid A for the student who worshiped at the feet of his shitty dad sneakers and cuffed khakis.

After that day in his office, I went home and listened to Shawn Colvin's "I Don't Know Why" over and over and over again until my roommates pounded on the door and asked me to turn it off. But I was grieving, and the words of the song rang through my body much more than the lyrics to "Cinnamon Girl" ever had. After weeks of listening to Neil Young, it felt good to come back home: "I don't know why, but somewhere dreams come true. And I don't know where, but there will be a place for you."

I could only be a dreamer of pictures and a chaser of moonlight if I came wrapped in a package that Alan wanted to open. I would've loved to have been his anything girl—Uptown Girl, Good-Time Girl, even his Working Girl—but that was never going to happen. He wanted a Cinnamon Girl, and and I would always be Big Red.

NINE

WIFE CAMP

Below is an essay written in an upper-level intensive writing class while I was a student at Brigham Young University. Out of respect for the Good-Time Girl I was then and remain now, the words have been transcribed exactly as they were originally written.

Husbands!! Feeling threatened by an equal partnership? Intimidated by a competent mate? Have we got the solution for you! We, the company of Submissive & Sons, have met the call of domineering husbands everywhere. In order to combat the rising problem of women with personalities, our company has developed an intensive course that subdues the assertive wife: WIFE CAMP.

For a mere fee of $99.95, you can enroll an outspoken spouse, and six weeks later, return home with the Barbie doll of your dreams. Really! It's that simple.

Do you fear your wife is more knowledgeable than you, and runs the risk of showing you up in public? Then this program is for you. Our course begins with rigorous brainwashing by qualified specialists that can muddle the keenest mind. Your wife may enter a genius, but she will leave reciting nothing more than her name, favorite color, and dress size. You never again will be subject to the humbling effects of actually learning something from your wife. Our counselors have been specially instructed to command all incoming wives to only respond when spoken to and train them to smile and giggle at every comment you make. It is a husband's dream come true.

Is your wife putting on extra weight? Never fear. Our strict diet of bread and water will whittle away unwanted pounds, and unappealing cellulite. Never again will you be repulsed or embarrassed by your wife's appearance; she will return a new woman that you will be proud to take out in public.

Is your wife asserting her opinion and constantly demanding respect? This problem, too, can be solved by our unique WIFE CAMP. After six weeks of constant belittling and abuse, your once confident wife will transform into a gracious, compliant hostess, eager to serve you and your friends.

Is there a high school reunion or important party coming up in your calendar? Don't take the chance of being scorned by your colleagues. Plan ahead, and enroll your wife today. Don't spend another football season fetching your own beer and pretzels. Instead, be the envy of all your buddies by displaying her new waitressing skills at the Super Bowl.

If she is enrolled before December 15, you will receive an extra bonus of a private session with our critically acclaimed make-over magician. After carefully consulting you on the style and look you want your new wife to achieve, we will transfer your once dowdy wife into a specimen that will look impressive on your arm.

The results of WIFE CAMP cannot be numbered. It is the perfect gift for a fellow husband experiencing frustration with a wife that simply won't *obey. Our program is 100% guaranteed. If not fully satisfied, we will either refund the cost, or invite you to enroll your wife again in another session, free of charge. Register her now and you will also receive an autographed instructional manual to keep her in line once you take her home. For the more disobedient of wives, leashes and collars can be purchased at whole-sale costs.*

Hurry and reserve a slot! Don't let another day go by where you are subjected to her views and forced to acknowledge her presence. WIFE CAMP is the solution to every man's marital burden. Isn't it about time you were in complete control? Create the woman you deserve.

Call now to reserve a position for your wife—spaces are limited.

TEN

DEEP ERUPTION

Three days into my marriage, I realized it was doomed. It all started when my husband farted in Maui. It might seem like a stupid thing, but in that offensive moment, he not only broke wind, he also broke the reverie. It wasn't the first red flag, or even the first flatulence, but it was the first moment that I felt a flash of despair from which I never fully recovered.

When I first met my husband, Billy, I was smitten almost immediately. Mostly because he was the first boy to ask me out who was a real candidate for marriage. I was twenty-four years old, living in Huntington Beach, and frustrated with the casual dating scene in my LDS Singles Ward. I'd spent my youth pining for a mate, but I had mostly been met with disappointment. The guys that liked me inevitably gave me the "ick," and the boys that I felt drawn to always put me directly into the friendzone. When Billy rolled into town, he asked me out the very night he moved in. He was over six feet tall, from a good family, and he was Mormon. My fate was sealed. He was exactly what I thought I was looking for. I was feeling pressure from every side of my life to get married. To pretend to be choosy when I was already teetering on the brink of spinsterhood would've been sudden death. I was into him; he was into me. What more did we need?

We were engaged less than three months after our first date and married within three more. Our entire courtship from hello to honeymoon was less than nine months in total. We hadn't cooked together, slept together, or lived together yet, but I still called him my soulmate and best friend, hoping that by saying the words I would somehow manifest them into reality.

On the day of our wedding reception, we were in a glass gazebo overlooking the Pacific Ocean at Turtle Bay Resort on Oahu. It was picture-perfect and projected the fairy tale I wanted to have. Our family and friends were staying at the hotel, but we wanted to spend our first night together across the island. We rented a white stretch limousine to take us from Turtle Bay to the Ihilani Resort, about twenty-five minutes away.

Once we cut the cake and said our goodbyes, everything happened pretty quickly. As the car pulled up to whisk us to newlywed bliss, Billy hustled me into the limousine. He chivalrously opened the door and had me climb inside first. But instead of shutting the door and going around to the other side of the car to get in himself, he began to climb in after me. The farther I was pushed into the limo, the more I realized that the final moment of my big day was quickly slipping away. This was my last chance to wave goodbye to everyone, to bid farewell to my former life, and to have a picturesque moment of myself in a white gown and floral crown waving out the window of a white limousine.

Acting on instinct, I popped my head halfway out the door as Billy nudged me farther down the seat. I hoped he would see my physical block, acknowledge his mistake, exit the car, and move around to the other side. But instead, he said loudly, "What are you doing?"

I felt immediately embarrassed, but I hadn't yet learned to swallow what I wanted for my husband's sake, so I persisted and replied, "I want to wave goodbye."

He pushed the door farther open with the back of his outside leg and sighed as I crouched on all fours and stuck my head out. This obviously didn't work well and was not the graceful picture I had imagined. Realizing how dumb I looked, I surrendered and retreated inside as Billy clambered all the way in.

I felt stifled and cheated—and also ashamed that I had been so self-involved on our special day as we departed. Who was I to imagine a Cinderella wave out the carriage window? I was mostly disappointed that Billy hadn't picked up on what I needed. But I didn't want to start my marriage with a fight, so I blocked out the moment entirely. I was only reminded of it when I saw one of the final pictures of our wedding day. In the photo, I am desperately begging for a final moment of recognition on all fours just seconds before my benefactor slams the door on my old life and traps me inside the tinted windows of his world.

When we arrived at the hotel, I walked into the lobby in my wedding gown. Billy was still wearing his tux, but amid all the tourists checking in and milling around, I felt conspicuous. It was not the fairy tale I had imagined. We took the elevator up to our room and immediately changed into our swimsuits. There was no carrying me over the threshold and throwing me onto the bed. It was all very routine. I had Billy help me unzip my dress, but even that simple act felt strangely intimate and awk-

ward. We had basically gotten married in order to have sex without sin-
ning, but now that we had full permission, it seemed frighteningly banal.
We got married for this? I went into the bathroom to change; it seemed
completely foreign to take my clothes off in front of him even though
he was my husband. I put on a blue bikini with a bright pink sarong and
walked back into the room, my wedding dress in my arms. Billy looked
up from where he was sitting and gazed at me for a second.

"You're beautiful," he said, like he was seeing me for the first time.

Instead of feeling flattered, I felt slightly irritated with the way he
said it, and my mind flooded with questions: Was he only just noticing?
Why had he married me? Why did these words sound so foreign coming from his lips? I don't think he had ever told me that I was beautiful
before, and I'm positive I never heard it again after that day.

Our relationship wasn't based on baby talk and compliments, and
I thought that made it strong—even if it was less sweet. But I thought
wrong. I didn't know him at all, and he didn't know me either.

We swam in the lagoon and conquered my virginity with passion,
but despair was just around the corner. The rumblings of the sleeping
volcano had begun.

The following day, when we began the second leg of our honeymoon, Billy made sure to allot ample time to say goodbye to the
resort's bus driver. He had been so quick to load into the limousine
with no more than a desultory wave but was the king of small talk once
we were on the complimentary airport shuttle.

That afternoon, after a quick flight to Kahului Airport in Maui, we
had little time to waste. Once we landed, we planned to rent a car so
that we could take ourselves on self-guided tours around the island.
We had only allotted two nights in Maui because we were planning on

spending the bulk of our honeymoon on a third island where a friend through Billy's family had donated their Marriott time-share. It was on the island of Molokai, which went from being a deserted leper colony to a beautifully untouched paradise the second we heard the price: FREE.

In Maui, the number-one must-see attraction is the Haleakala Crater. Renowned for its views at dawn, Haleakala was on the top of my Hawaiian wish list. It was important for me to see because once we got to Molokai, the activities would be limited to their number one tourist attraction: the Kalaupapa Leper Colony. But seeing Haleakala at dawn would make up for all of that.

In order to make it to the crest of the crater by sunrise, we had to wake up early. *Really* early. The-butt-crack-of-dawn early. Four a.m. to be exact. And Billy didn't want to.

Sure, he was open to seeing the volcano, but he couldn't understand why it was so important to see the view at sunrise. To him, sleeping in seemed like a much better option.

He can't be serious, I thought. *Come on, man. We are young, we are in love, and we are on our honeymoon in Maui. We are going to see a goddamn sunrise on the top of a volcano in one of the most idyllic locations on the Earth!*

Waking up early hadn't even occurred to me as a deterrent. Of course we were waking up early. How else do you see a sunrise?

I didn't want to seem abrupt or bossy about our early start time, so I put together a plan. I carefully set my alarm on the lowest decibel possible. I planned to wake up a few minutes early and use the time to gently and lovingly wake Billy with honeymoon kisses and gentle nudges, all in the hopes that he would change his mind about the early wake-up call. My biggest fear was incorrectly timing the morning's operation. The last thing I wanted to do was force Billy to wake up, drive two hours, and still miss the sunrise because we had been stuck in line at the entrance for a minute too long.

I hoped that once Billy saw it, he'd be grateful he hadn't slept in, and he'd thank me for pushing him to wake up early. But if I timed it wrong, we'd have woken up early for nothing, and I would be screwed. I'd have to compensate for my failed plan for the rest of our vacation— perhaps even the rest of our lives. I'd likely lose the right or privilege to suggest any other tourist activity for the rest of the honeymoon. Something inside me, even then, knew that my opinion only mattered if it was the only correct choice. I didn't have enough experience with Billy to prove it, but I had a hunch that it was his way or the highway for most things. Deep down, I felt like it was essential that I was always right, because as soon as I was wrong, I feared that one mistake or misstep would be remembered forever and then be used to question my credibility in every single situation moving forward.

The night before, I hardly slept. I was so scared that I'd sleep through the alarm. As soon as I heard its near-silent ring, I sidled off the bed as quietly as possible. I dressed in the bathroom in the dark. Then, I turned on the warm bathroom light to create a slow, ambient sidelight, a careful, natural circadian awakening. I crept into the darkness with the light-footedness of a spy and crossed the room to our bed.

"Billy? Babe? It's time to wake up," I cooed.

Nothing.

I caressed his shoulder and gently shook his side.

"Billy? Babe, we have to wake up so we can go see the sunrise!"

He snorted and shifted but ultimately shook me off.

In my head I pleaded, *Please just wake up. Please don't make me be this person. I want you to be the one that's excited about this road trip. I'm supposed to be the diva, not you.*

But we were married now, and I wanted to see the sunrise together as a couple. More than that, I wanted to be married to a man who wanted to see the sunrise. So, whatever it took to get there, I needed to make it happen without acknowledging the creeping fear that my husband and I were incompatible. Was it possible that we would never appreciate or share the same sacred moments?

I pushed his shoulder more strongly and said a little louder, "Come on, Billy. If we don't leave soon, we'll miss it!"

I kept my voice high-pitched and chipper like an exercise instructor at a senior care facility. I didn't want to speak down to him, so I had to carefully toe the line between coddling and condescension.

Eventually, he half sat up and placed his stockinged feet on the floor next to the bed, his shoulders slumped and his head still hanging low. He wasn't wearing any pajamas, just his temple garments, top and bottoms. They were too big for his lanky frame: the neck hung loosely and the shoulder lines hung limply two or three inches below his shoulders accentuating the shrug of his back. They were loose around his thighs and slightly saggy in the butt. This was his honeymoon lingerie. He felt absolutely comfortable seducing his new bride in his dingy magic underwear.

Billy continued to show no form of life, so I continued to encourage him: "Are you excited? I'm so excited! Haleakala, babe!!"

He just sat there. Nothing. No response. No movement. It was so silent in fact that, for a second, I thought he had fallen back asleep while sitting on the edge of the bed. And then, a sound broke through the void, bleating through the silence.

First, a soft hollow tharump . . . followed by an extended percussion of jackhammer beats. A momentary pause and then a quick six or seven solid rat-a-tat-tats followed.

I stood there in the dusky bathroom light and tried to process what I had just heard. Was that a fart? Had Billy just ripped a "Get-out-and-walk-Donald" in our honeymoon suite? The sound seemed to have come from his direction, but I saw no movement. If it had indeed come from his body, I would've expected him to rise three or four inches above the mattress from the sheer wind power, or at least for the sheets to vibrate and tremble with the Brownian motion of it all.

"Was that you?" I asked. I couldn't even believe that I was asking this of my groom of three days.

He looked over at me blandly and then, without blinking, stared straight into my eyes and let out a second steady staccato stream of farts.

I laughed out of pure shock.

"Are you serious right now?" I was flummoxed.

"I get gas when I have to wake up early," he offered smugly.

I swear I saw a glimmer of rebellion pass through his eyes. A flash of "I told you I didn't want to do this." Even though he was up, he wasn't going to make this easy.

In that moment—amidst the flatulence—I felt like I had a choice: I could feign horror, up the ante, and make such a scene that he would never dare defiantly fart like that in my presence again, or I could be the cool girl, plug my nose and roll with it. If I had been able to see into my future, I might've known that neither choice would work out. I wasn't the cool girl, and I didn't want to roll with it. And there was no scene I could create, no ante too high, to change or adjust his behavior. So instead I handed him his clothes and shoes and tried to make a few jokes. This was my go-to. If I could be funny enough about a situation, I could change the reality of it. Humor in hard moments was my crutch, but I didn't expect to have to resort to my crutches so early in my marriage.

"Come on! The sunrise won't wait for us. Let's go! Once we get to the car you can fart all you want as long as the windows are down."

But the farting was just the beginning of my punishments that day. Since I apparently *loved* getting up early and clearly he didn't, Billy volunteered me to drive. Our first road trip as a married couple and I was the conductor, cruise director, and chauffeur. It was an hour of Hawaiian highway and then a climb up the mountain on difficult switchbacks in the dark, but I reluctantly agreed. I wanted to say, "Of course I can drive the goddamn car, but I don't want to, and more than that, I want YOU to not want me to." *Isn't the man supposed to drive?* I thought. *Shouldn't I focus on the scenery or play navigator or do my makeup and file my nails?* This was not the road trip I had imagined.

I wanted him to lead, and then, while he was leading, I wanted to surprise him with my competence. *I can do it all, but only if you can't.* Still yet another part of me convinced myself that I loved that I *could* do it all, and I didn't want to apologize for it or shrink my capabilities down in order to feel taken care of.

So I begrudgingly got behind the wheel of our rented economy car, and I drove. Of course, I couldn't listen to music because Billy needed quiet to continue sleeping. If I drove fast or stopped too abruptly or took a sharp turn, he'd loll his snoring head to the side and chastise me: "Geez, babe. Can you not?"

It's hard to describe how that drive to Haleakala killed my hope and, in many ways, broke my spirit. But, from the moment our sedan pulled out of the porte cochere, I felt like we were doomed. It wasn't the explosive farts; it wasn't the economy car; it wasn't the star-crossed schedules. ("Did you hear about Billy and Heather? They split up. He *hated* waking up early and she just couldn't shake her love of sunrises.") The fissure at the heart of our marriage was that I wanted to have a special moment in a specific kind of way that Billy neither wanted nor cared to share, and he was doing everything he could to sabotage it.

Billy slept and snored the entire two-hour drive to the crater. I felt like a hired driver or, worse, a camp counselor on a field trip he didn't want to take. I woke him up when we reached the top, and he didn't even move his seat from the reclined position. He just kind of hiked his body up long enough to look outside the window at the streaming ribbons of blue and orange and pink and yellow emanating from below the clouds, illuminating the peaks of the volcano. It was spectacular: a wonder of the world, a once-in-a-lifetime moment. Billy gazed at the horizon for less than a minute before he lay back down and closed his eyes. I had never felt lonelier in my entire life.

Was it really too much to ask to see the sunrise from the top of a volcano in Maui? We were blessed to be in Hawaii period. Waking up to watch the sun peak over the Pacific felt almost obligatory. Like it was the very least we could do to make the most of a trip so few ever have the privilege of experiencing.

The little girl who chased the frogs at the motel pool in San Bernardino would have jumped for joy at the thought of seeing the world awaken atop a dormant volcano on a tropical island paradise. I used to dream about times like these, and now that I was living it, I couldn't help but notice how very different my dreams were from reality. Sure, I had traded the crusty pool light and tiny frogs for the rising sun and a real-life prince, but if he was going to sleep through the entire thing, was it even worth it?

I sat there, looking out at the landscape before me, and pushed the resentment and the anger and the disappointment I was feeling down deeper in my heart. Sure, the sunrise was beautiful. Sure, I was glad I had woken up. Sure, I was glad I was married. But nothing about that morning reflected the special moment I had hoped it would be, and the fact that Billy had sabotaged it all, whether consciously or not, was too much to bear.

A cold volcano can stay dormant for years, but it'll erupt eventually.

ELEVEN

CORNFLAKE GIRL

If music be the food of love, play on! I remember the first time I saw this phrase on a decal above the hot-food bar at Whole Foods and felt seen. Music, Food, Love, Shakespeare! A symphony of delights. And music was the great connector. From my first concert with my dad (Bruce Springsteen), to my first concert without a chaperone (Bon Jovi), to my first concert alone (Tracy Chapman), music has been a constant life force flowing through my veins. I consider myself born with a musical ear, though no one has ever confirmed it. I was an accomplished classical pianist, an amateur songwriter, and, above all else, an aficionado of the art. I loved music. I loved the latest and greatest, the oldies, the alternatives, the B-sides, the bootlegs. Music was a window into cultures and experiences and people that I would never encounter in real life; by listening to music, I was effortlessly transported to worlds I could never access otherwise.

I was an eighties baby and I joined every CD subscription service that Columbia House and RCA offered. Never canceling on time, never paying on time, never returning any of the unwanted CDs. I wanted them all. I needed REO Speedwagon's "Can't Fight This Feeling" to explain to Clayton in the ninth grade why I wanted to be more than friends. Morp came and went my sophomore year without a date to the dance, and it was "Love's Recovery" by the Indigo Girls that helped me process the pain. When I dreamed of my future husband, I heard Marc Cohn singing "True Companion." I processed gender roles with Dar Williams's "When I Was a Boy," and, as I detailed earlier, I cried my eyes out to Shawn Colvin's "I Don't Know Why" when Alan Smithson, my instructor at BYU, preempted my declaration of love by confiding in me that he was interested in my skinny, brunette classmate.

Her lyrics, "And I don't know why—I don't know anything at all—but if there were no music, then I would not get through," resonated in me, and I reflected on the soundtrack of my life, and how the music I cherished had always been able to speak to my conflicted heart and soul in a way that nothing else could.

My CD collection by the time I was in my early twenties was probably close to a thousand. I had been collecting them from the moment I received my first Discman as a Christmas gift at the age of thirteen. After our wedding in Hawaii, Billy and I moved in together in Huntington Beach, California. I wanted to make our house a home, but I still wanted to keep everything that was important to me. I bought all of the special CD storage cabinets and disguised them around the house as accessory furniture. The cases and liner notes took up a lot of space, but they were a part of the ritual for me, and I liked to have them at the ready. I'd select a jacket, pop the CD in my fancy five-disc player, and gingerly pull the tiny, folded pamphlet from the plastic case. I would read every word. Look at every picture. Study the supplementary info.

I'd note the guest artists, the backup singers. I'd look for patterns in percussionists and songwriters and recording studios. It was before the internet, and if you wanted to look up the lyrics to a song, the CD insert was really your only option. Line by line, precept by precept, I built my collection one by one, and I treasured each CD for the music and treasured each CD jacket for the jewels within.

If Billy couldn't tell I loved music just by living with me, he could tell by looking at my CD collection. It was extensive and impressive. And yet still unobtrusive. None of my friends had ever remarked on the space my collection took up, or even questioned the placement of the decorative furniture that stored everything. I assumed Billy would cherish it as much as I did, mostly because it required absolutely nothing of him. But I was wrong.

The first thing I learned once I was finally married and living with a man was all the ways I'd been doing things wrong. Every day, it seemed like Billy had a new way for me to improve my life. He had a knack for being helpful in what I can only describe as the *worst* possible way. Occasionally, I would fall asleep while scrolling on my phone, and it would drop into the space between the mattress and the nightstand. I never complained about it, or groaned about it, or even gave it a second thought. I just looked for my phone, and if I couldn't find it, assumed it had fallen under the bed. But it bugged Billy whenever he saw me pawing on the ground looking for it. So he decided to fix the problem once and for all. He took a tube of Gorilla Glue and adhered two giant squares of Velcro onto the phone and onto the nightstand. It was a ridiculous solution. Why would I ever want to hold a phone with Velcro glued on it? If it had been an option, he would've glued Velcro to my hand, as long as it prevented me from losing my phone. When

I demonstrated to him that I had to use both hands to pry the phone off the Velcro—sending the phone flying across the room—he realized maybe his perfect solution wasn't all that perfect . . . for me.

This was just one of the innumerable ways he sought to improve my quality of life, and I constantly walked the line of being outwardly appreciative while being inwardly annoyed. I should have been more wary than I was when I arrived home from work one evening and saw him in the parking lot of our complex, throwing a file box into the community dumpster. Instead of questioning him, I followed him inside, waiting to see what appliance cords had been zip-tied into place or how many standing fans had been purchased to create white noise and air flow. He seemed giddier than usual and gestured to a giant electric-blue plastic binder on the coffee table.

"Check it out," he said.

I sat on our black leather couch and pulled the binder onto my lap. It was enormous. It must have weighed close to twenty-five pounds.

"What is it?" I asked.

I noticed the Case Logic logo on the cover and flipped it open. It was a CD storage binder with thin plastic sleeves divided into squares. At first glance, I wasn't sure what I was looking at. Tom Petty and the Heartbreakers, Red Hot Chili Peppers, Shania Twain, Dave Matthews Band. I hardly recognized the CDs laid bare without their covers, but I still recognized the album names.

Billy must be showing me his CD collection, I imagined. *Not too shabby, Billy. I can support this.*

I flipped the page and saw eight more impressive CDs, segregated and stripped down, on display in their flimsy plastic coverings.

And then I saw it: Tori Amos's *Under the Pink*. The matte silver finish made this particular CD stand out from the others. Tori Amos? The angsty feminist singer/songwriter that composed lyrics about her strict religious upbringing and sexual awakening? These weren't Billy's CDs. They were *mine*. My mouth went dry. I tried to process why *my* CDs were in this monstrosity of a binder. The lyrics of the song "Cornflake Girl" pounded in my ears: *"This is not really . . . this this this is not really happening."*

Billy reached down and started flipping the pages rapidly, oblivious to the panic rising in my throat.

"Look at this! I organized as many CDs as I could in one place. Three-hundred-thirty-six-CD storage capacity."

He laughed proudly at his resourcefulness.

I was paralyzed, frozen in time.

"When did you do this? You didn't have to do this for me. No, really, you didn't have to organize my entire CD collection," I protested.

"Well, it's not really *organized*," Billy responded. "Not like into categories or anything. I just took all the CDs out of their cases and put them in the plastic sleeves."

The world stopped spinning. The *cases*. I gulped and tried to maintain my composure. I looked around the room, desperately. *Where were the cases?* As soon as I asked myself the question, the image of Billy hoisting the giant file box into the blue dumpster from earlier flashed through my mind. I felt nauseated, but instead of dry heaving into the blue Case Logic binder, I smiled at him.

"What did you do with all the cases?" I asked as meekly as I could.

"I tossed 'em," he said proudly. "You still have a few empty storage sleeves at the back just in case you need to add more, but honestly you have too many as it is."

Somewhere between "I tossed 'em," and "You have too many," I left my body and began observing the scene outside of myself. I was losing it. I tried to concentrate on keeping my cool: *Deep breath. Find out where he tossed the cases. You can put them all back. It's a hassle, but it's not the end of the world. Don't be a bitch. He was trying to be nice.*

"Oh shoot, I know it's dumb, but I love the cases. Isn't that silly? I'd like to save them if it's possible. Out of curiosity, where did you toss them?" I stood up and began pacing back and forth, rambling aloud and not listening for a response. I had boarded a runaway train of panic and excuses, and it had clearly left the station. I started for the front door and for the dumpster beyond.

He called after me, "They're gone, Heather. I threw them away. That's the whole point of the storage system. It only works without the cases." But it was too late; I was already out the door.

He followed me out to the dumpster despite my protests and pandering. The sun had set and the streetlights gave a hazy glow through the evening fog settling over Huntington Beach. I was barely tall enough to peer over the metal edge of the dumpster, and as soon as I did, the scent of all the garbage whacked me fully in the face. September in Southern California could turn any sanitation container into a stomach-churning stew. I tried to ignore the stench.

"I'm going to get a step stool and grab some of the covers that are on top," I suggested casually.

Billy immediately recoiled.

"No way. No. That's just crazy. Come on. They are in the garbage. It's disgusting and you don't need the stupid covers anyway. They take up too much space. I don't know why you're making this such a big deal."

I didn't know why I was making it such a big deal either. But I couldn't help it. I felt like my heart was being ripped out of my chest. I could feel sobs forming internally, but I pushed away the impulse to cry. Instead, I silenced myself and agreed with him. What was the point? It was a zero-sum game. Even if I won this battle, I had already lost the war.

"You're right. I'm being crazy. This is stupid. I'm sorry."

My forced retreat was too late and not genuine enough. I had snubbed his thoughtful act of love and was swirling in a cloud of shame and rage and sadness. The night was ruined even though we both pretended we had moved on. Billy's feelings were hurt, and my feelings were so repressed, I was scared that if I opened my mouth, I'd bray like a donkey, screaming and crying. Not being able to form actual words, just sounds of defeat.

Later that night, after Billy had fallen asleep to his whirring fans of white noise, I snuck outside to the parking lot armed with a barstool from the kitchen. It was dark out, and every passing car blinded me with its headlights. I pushed back the shame of what I was about to do, peered into the giant dumpster, and saw my collection of CD jackets scattered and strewn among Styrofoam food containers, greasy kitchen garbage bags, and crumpled cereal boxes. These were my treasures, my lyrics, my literary accompaniment to the audible experience. They were the heart of my collection. As essential to me as the music that came from the CDs. More so in some ways because they were tangible souvenirs of my independent life and the decade that created me, both of which were soon to be collector's items.

There was no way I could rescue and restore everything that had been thrown away without looking like a crazy person, but more than that, there was no way for me to attempt to recover everything and still pretend that Billy had done nothing to upset me. And less than full recovery would've been a futile effort. If I was only able to save a few jackets, the ones I left behind would haunt me forever.

Under the Pink was under the garbage pile now. And while I was grieving the loss of the liner notes and cover art, I was also grieving something much bigger. I had married a man who didn't see or appreciate the things I loved most about myself. He saw my collection as a nuisance and an eyesore; he saw my passion for music as something that he would make fit into his world in his way. I was a liner note to his CD, and as such, to him, I was disposable.

How did I not see this before? What type of mental gymnastics had allowed me to blind myself to the reality of our relationship? I hated him for what he had done, but I hated myself more for marrying him, because now I was stuck. If I wanted kids, it would have to be with him. We were married in the temple after all, so divorce wasn't really an option. But I didn't want to be married to him. I didn't want to raise kids with him. I didn't even want to spend the night in the same room as him. There was no escape hatch, but there was also no way forward. If I couldn't be honest about my CD covers, how could I be honest about my broken heart?

My marriage was built to see the world from his vantage point, and it was irrelevant how his perspectives limited or inhibited mine, or how his governance came at the cost of my independence. The CDs were just the beginning. But it felt like he had discarded one of the most precious parts of me and didn't feel bad about doing it. And that pattern would be forever repeated.

I had gotten myself here, and I hated myself for it. I had believed in the love songs I had listened to over and over, and I believed that the music would somehow get me through. What worked so beautifully in theory fell apart in practice. Who I wanted him to be was not who he was, and who he wanted me to be was an even bigger disappointment. I feared that we had gotten married for all the wrong reasons. I wanted him to become passionate about what I was passionate about and to cherish what I cherished. Because that's what I expected love to do; at least that's what all the love songs promised. But it was a beautiful lie. We didn't know or love each other in the ways we needed. And worse, we fell in love with versions of each other that we couldn't sustain.

If I had known our fate, I never would've knelt down in the temple on our wedding day and pledged myself to him for time and all eternity. I would've told myself that it's better to be alone than to be misunderstood, and the hardest truths are the ones you refuse the longest to see.

If he had seen me for who I was that day, he would have helped me save all of my CDs and their precious cases. He would have wrapped his arms around me and listened to the music of Tori Amos to soothe my soul. He would have seen me in the way I longed to be seen. He would have known I *"never was a cornflake girl."*

TWELVE

THE H IS SILENT

orry about your name," my mom whispered once we were safely inside the inner vestibule.

I was twenty-one years old and "going through" the LDS Temple for the first time. We called it "going through" the temple because the endowment ceremony required you to "go through" several stages of dress and undress, several rooms with different purposes, and several rituals in order to complete the process and "receive" your endowment. Once you went through the temple for yourself, you returned frequently to go through the temple for other people—more specifically, dead people, who were unable to complete the rituals while they lived on Earth. A significant part of the LDS faith is believing that it's your duty and privilege to act as a proxy for the dead and complete these rituals for them. The sacred process requires you to adopt a new name, a secret name, a name whispered quietly in your ear so that only you can hear it and that you are immediately instructed afterward to never reveal unless prompted. Everything about the secret name implies that it is individual, predestined, assigned by God and as unbreakable as the fourteen-digit security codes that your browser prompts you to use. The secrecy of the name was emphasized so much that when my mom even referenced knowing mine, I felt actual fear flash through my body.

How did she know my temple name when *I* wasn't even sure what it was?

It had only been about three hours since the name was given to me. The name had been whispered by the same temple volunteer who had placed a round orange sticker on the lapel of my rented white dress, alerting all the other volunteers that this was my first endowment ceremony and I might be needing a little extra help. All newbies are adorned with this fluorescent orange sticker, almost like a *Rocky Horror Picture Show* lipstick "V" on the forehead.

The temple volunteer was in her early seventies, and her gray hair hung limply around her face. Her eyes were red-rimmed, watery, and crystalline blue, unclouded by cataracts or glaucoma. I wanted to look away, but I was scared that if I didn't keep eye contact, she would think it was because I wasn't worthy to be there. It had only been a week since I'd been flirting with boys in the shoe department where I worked at Nordstrom, pulling the cigar from their mouths and posing seductively for photos with a disposable camera. Could she tell by looking at me that I had a taste for temptation? I imagined that if I snickered or glanced away, I'd be revealed, and she'd reach underneath her temple robe and pull out a fluorescent orange whistle that matched my sticker, and let out a shrill alarm signaling she'd found an imposter. When she whispered my new name to me, I was so focused on looking sincere that I wasn't really even listening. I heard her make a sound, but it didn't register as an actual word, let alone a *name*. Immediately, after she said it, she looked me straight in the eyes and began to give me the warning and penalties that would befall me if I were ever to reveal it. There wasn't a spare moment for me to say, "Huh? Can you repeat that?" She made it clear that she was using her serious voice—her "I'm not mad yet but don't fucking push me" voice when she spoke. She explained that this sacred new name was my personal private token that I would need to remember in order to get into Heaven. (*Fuck! I'm not even sure I could repeat it!*) It was also the name by which my future husband would call me forth in order to get married and the password that, at the final resurrection, would qualify me to pass through the veil and join my family with God in the highest of glories: the Celestial Kingdom.

This was the first covenant I was making in the temple and I had already blown it. With all these levels of secrecy and confusion, how did my *mom* know it? And I knew she wasn't bluffing, it had to be the same name, because she knew that it was . . . well . . . awful?

When the temple volunteer whispered it to me, I wasn't sure I had even heard it correctly. It sounded as if she had been clearing her throat in preparation for the big announcement, but when no other words or sounds followed . . . I realized that that was it. My new name sounded like a phlegm wad; I wasn't sure I could even spell it phonetically.

This was the name. The name God knew me as. My temple name; the only name that really mattered. It was the sacred sign and token that everyone in Heaven would know me by for eternity, and it was bad. Next-level *bad*. Like if a teacher saw the name on the roll for attendance, their-bowels-would-be-filled-with-compassion *bad*. What-were-the-parents-thinking *bad*. Only tradition could keep a name like this alive, and only someone cruel would willingly give it to their daughter. No loving Father in Heaven would bestow such a name on a girl who already felt big-boned, bawdy, and embarrassingly white. But here I was, and he had . . . and I didn't know how I was going to spin it.

It sounded like a rural version of Gesundheit with fewer syllables and consonants. It was not a name I had ever read in the baby-name books I had pored over during my doll-playing days. Names were very important to me during these sessions. I would set up a makeshift orphanage in my playroom with cribs lining the walls. All the baby dolls were placed according to their made-up refugee nation and dutifully named based on the international section of *The Best Baby Name Book Ever*. It was a cerulean paperback that my mom had purchased during her sixth and final pregnancy. That book was my baby-naming bible, and I made sure that the Swedes and the Bulgarians and the sweet Latvian orphans that I rescued were all named something from the Top Ten Most Popular List according to their country of origin: Svetlana, Claudia, Bogdonna. I wanted each name to roll off my tongue and match the doll it was assigned to. I wanted the names to have a meaning that represented their hardship, but also their potential. Names were important, and as a kind but stern orphanage matron, I knew that better than anybody.

When it came time to naming my own children, I pored over my choices, counting syllables and vowels, considering iambic pentameter, middle names, last names. I accounted for monograms, alphabetized lists, future job applications, and college essays. I visualized the name on a cursive patch on the back of a letterman jacket, in a dance program, and in different fonts. Sure it had zing in Arial Black, but it was a jumbled mess in Zapfino! I wanted a name that could be used to model embroidery on Pottery Barn pillow shams and preschool backpacks. A name that presented a thrilling surprise when it surfaced on a personalized miniature license plate at a Midwestern roadside gift shop: "Mom! Mom! There's a *Jillian!*"

Surely the good Lord cared at least as much as I did about his own children's temple names?

But apparently he didn't because my endowment ceremony began with a congested cough rather than a beautiful, meaningful name. The only solace I found was in the fact that the name was a secret that would not be revealed until the moment I faced Heavenly Father Himself at the pearly gates.

"What did you say?" I asked my mom.

"I said 'sorry about your new name,'" she repeated with a cringe and a grimace. She rubbed my back consolingly.

I was dressed in full priesthood robes, a fig-leaf apron tied around my waist, with my family and friends surrounding me in similar attire. We stood in the only room in the temple where we were allowed to discuss the most sacred and secret parts of what we had just experienced. If I needed clarification on anything, this would be the time to ask. But even with all the rules suspended, I still felt uncomfortable that my mom was claiming to know my temple name. So I lied.

"Oh, I love my name. It's beautiful and totally meaningful to me."

My mom pulled back, her chin suspiciously dropping into her neck: "Huh? Really?" she asked skeptically. "You must've gotten a different one than us, then." She scampered off as her white priesthood robes swished against her knee-high nylons.

They all have the same name as me? I thought. *How did* that *work?* But instead of questioning the divinity of the naming ceremony, I felt immediately stricken with the fact that I had just told my first lie after being washed clean just like I had after my baptism at age eight. I couldn't stay perfect for even five fucking minutes. Perhaps even more damning, I had chosen to lie in the Celestial Room of God's Holy Temple which had to carry extra penalties in Hell. I was sure of it.

It would be at least twenty years before I would learn how my mom knew my secret name even before I did. We of course never spoke of it again once we left the temple that day, and I didn't dare bring it up in casual conversation with friends or even church leaders. The secrecy and shame kept everyone quiet. But what my mom knew that I would learn later is that every single patron attending the temple that day was given the same temple name. There was no divination or individuality about it. The Lord has way too many children to labor over a regional or universal temple name book, let alone the Top Ten names from any specific country. He is omniscient and omnipotent, but his procedure for assigning temple names is surprisingly rudimentary. Across the globe, in every operating temple, there are two universal names assigned each day: one for men and one for women. I was going through the temple for myself, so the name was especially significant. My mom and everyone else were going through the temple as a proxy for our ancestors, so they were less invested. Her personal temple name had been assigned years prior when she received her first endowment. And based on the way she was judging my temple name, it was clear that she had gotten a good one, probably Mary or even Elizabeth.

Part of the ritual required us to whisper our name through a hole in a temple curtain while engaging in a secret handshake with a man on the other side. When it came time for me to do it, I looked over pleadingly at my helper. We made eye contact, and I swear I saw a flash of sympathy pass across her face as she whispered it in my ear. I cocked my head in confusion, and then, without breaking her gaze, I leaned toward the curtain and tried to mimic the sound she had just uttered. It seemed to do the trick, because he accepted my answer and unclasped my hand. I was still unsure of what I had said.

I told myself that God had selected my name because it sounded like it started with an H, and because Heather started with an H, God therefore knew me and loved me and was giving me a little wink from above. When I got home from the temple that day, I immediately looked for versions of the name in the Bible dictionary and index of the Book of Mormon. I stumbled upon one that looked like a match, and I was right! It started with an H.

My namesake was a prophetess from the Old Testament with a polarizing message to share with her people. Despite the difficulty, she bravely and dutifully declared God's warnings. But I didn't want a brave and dutiful name. I wanted something delicate, beautiful, and significant: Rachel. Ruth. Sarah. Hell, I would have even taken Boaz. At least something recognizable, pronounceable even. A name that people liked and remembered. Not something that sounded like a bodily function.

Maybe this whole religious thing wasn't really for me. You want to humble a headstrong Mormon girl, really kick her in the back of the knee? Just give her a shitty temple name.

I had always liked my birth name: Heather. It worked for me when I was young. It was sexy and flirty, had romantic undertones, and was distinctly feminine, all of which I assumed made me alluring to men. It had the potential to be seductive, but could still hold its own around a conference table. She might not be seated at the head of the boardroom, but a Heather could most definitely be a prom queen *and* a debate captain.

My biggest complaint with my birth name was that it was hard to translate into other languages. In French, the "th" sound is hard to pronounce and the "h" is always silent. So Heather is always distinctly American. It was also hard-pressed for nicknames. I had friends call me Heth and Heath and Heath Bar. For a brief period in high school, a friend started calling me Heatherkins or Kins, which resulted in me unfortunately giving myself that tag as a Snapchat username, an irrevocable mistake. I liked that Heatherkins sounded small, while Heath Bar reminded me of my size and my penchant for toffee.

I wanted my temple name to have the same appeal as my earthly name. But what I got was a turnoff! It could be a deal-breaker in the final moments of the game. On a woman's wedding day, her husband is given her temple name in advance, enabling him to call her by name through the spiritual veil and lead her into Heaven. She is never given his name, it's deemed unnecessary and too sacred, but he will always know hers. In some relationships, it's used as leverage to show just how close a woman is to her husband—"My husband told me his temple name. We tell each other everything!"—or how devout her partner purports to be—"My spouse would never share his name with me. He is obedient in all things!" When I got to the Celestial Room at the conclusion of my wedding ceremony, I half expected my husband to make a comment about my unfortunate temple name. However, he didn't seem to notice how bad it was. In fact, he didn't seem to remember my name at all. I didn't want to look petty, so I didn't mention it. For fear of having to reveal my own, I never had the courage to ask him to reveal his. And so my ugly name was never mentioned and quickly forgotten.

Years later, when we had returned home from a three-hour block of church meetings, my husband casually offered, "There's this guy in my Elders Quorum that I want to be friends with, but I feel uncomfortable around him because his real name is the same as my temple name."

"What?" I asked incredulously. "WHO?!"—immediately beginning to list the members' names in my head alphabetically.

"I'm not going to say, but it's just awkward."

It had never occurred to me that one might brush up against one's own temple name in the wild. Because the name is a secret never uttered for risk of death and damnation, it's not the type of nugget upon which you can build a conversation, let alone a relationship. With a name like mine, I doubted another dared roam the Earth.

I was devastated that I hadn't been bestowed with a name that could be perpetuated in our family lineage as a sort of nod to our ancestral trailings. I envisioned myself in Heaven declaring, "I'm Eve, born Heather. And you?" only to be met with an elated, "I'm also Eve, born Ruth!" We'd throw our haloed heads back and laugh, embracing and rejoicing in the glory that was ours to share in good faith and humor: "Mom! Mom! There's an *Eve*!"

With the slip of my husband's tongue, he had dramatically increased the odds of me *discovering* his temple name. Whoever had his same name was one of fifteen to twenty guys who regularly met in his Elders Quorum and had been in attendance the day of his confession. I was looking at Vegas odds, only this time, I was determined to beat the House (of the Lord).

I started by eliminating the obvious rejects: temple names for men were either based on the Bible, the Book of Mormon, or one of our modern day prophets, so Tyson, Larry, Colby, and Quinn were automatically out.

I knew his name couldn't be a nickname; I couldn't imagine the good Lord, even with all his good humor, designating anyone a Danny rather than Daniel, or a BJ rather than Benjamin. The name had to be in full form. KC, Mikey, and Lenny were out immediately.

But then it got slightly trickier—David, Aaron, John, Luke.

The more investigative questions I asked, the more he caught on to my curiosity, and he shut me down.

"I shouldn't have said anything," he said. "Just forget about it."

Matthew, Peter, James, Paul. These were all options, but they were too commonplace to cause him to feel awkward in their presence. It had to be an unusual name. I was befuddled and intrigued.

Then, weeks later, as we sat on our bench in sacrament meeting, I noticed him pulling at his collar as he watched the first counselor conduct the meeting. As they announced the first speaker, I saw my husband's cheeks flush and his Adam's apple jaunt up and down jaggedly in his throat. I looked at the program and, without thinking, said the opening speaker's name out loud. Not at normal volume, but loud enough to startle him and cause him to look over at me aghast.

He had given himself away.

I smiled menacingly while maintaining eye contact as I said the name again—whispering this time—barely containing the laughter and euphoria I felt at having figured it out.

No wonder he didn't want me to know. He was probably keeping it a secret not out of righteousness, but out of sheer embarrassment. It was bad. It was a name, like mine, that would never make it onto any Top Ten Baby Name lists anytime soon. A name so weird that even I was shocked to have run into it in modern times. Saying his secret name out loud felt so wrong, and yet so right.

For the first time since my temple name had been uttered, it all made sense. Maybe I had it wrong. Where else in the world, in what universe could two such names be any less star-crossed than ours? How could a *Shem* do anything but love a *Huldah?*

THIRTEEN

I DON'T WANT TO "DO EVERYTHING"

In a mad rush to get to church on time at nine o'clock one Sunday morning, I handed Ashley, our then six-month-old baby, to Billy, my husband, to hold while I gathered my last-minute things. She had been fed, bathed, dressed, and swaddled in appropriately reverent shades of blush and bashful for sacrament meeting. As I transferred her to his arms, I started to give him specific instructions about holding her, but I consciously choked down the words of warning. Seeing him dressed and ready to leave for church with his crisp white shirt and blue silk tie, cradling our baby daughter with a ribbon stuck to her head with a Q-tip dab of Karo syrup, overwhelmed me with familial bliss. He looked like the perfect father, holding our baby, and we looked like the perfect family. What could possibly go wrong?

After passing Ashley to her dad, I walked into the bathroom to put on my lipstick. Thirty seconds later, as soon as I clicked the lid back onto the tube, I heard a wail. My heart stopped. I ran into the adjoining bedroom at the same time as Billy, who burst in through the other door. In between us, face down on the carpet next to the bed, was Ashley, motionless and squalling. I fell to my knees and scooped her up, scanning for obvious injuries. Her face was purplish red and her cries were so furious they were coming out in short, loud spurts, followed by deafening silence. I thought she was going to pass out from her unceasing, breathless screams. My chest seized with a fear I had never felt before, and I desperately looked to Billy.

He was wild-eyed and frantic: "Is she okay? What happened?"

I was gut punched. *What happened?* Any moron could clearly see what happened. Our baby had fallen and landed on her face because her dad had propped her up on the bed. I was too scared to say it out loud. I wanted him to explain what had happened; to realize it, to feel it, and to fall on his knees with the same anguish that I had.

"I thought you were holding her," I groaned as I unfolded her blankets and tried to examine her tiny body.

I thought about the instructions I had choked down when I handed her off and how they might have saved us if I'd said them. Instead, I had gotten caught up in the moment. I had wanted to pretend that being a dad was the most natural thing in the world. Those words of maternal instinct were simple instructions you might give to a curious child, not the father of a baby. Saying them would have revealed the ugly truth about our relationship: "Billy, here's our baby. I need you to hold her for me. Hold her in your actual hands, and don't put her down. Do you understand? Can you promise me that?"

I hadn't said any of those things. Instead, I had just smiled and handed him the baby, trusting that he would be able to take the reins and parent like an equal partner, despite his lack of training.

"It doesn't make any sense," he said, dumbfounded. "I sat her down right here on the bed, and then I heard her screaming."

It doesn't make sense? It's called gravity. You balanced a baby on a raised platform bed. You'd barely left the room before she toppled right off the edge and two and a half feet down onto the carpet. It doesn't make sense? What doesn't make sense is why you set her down at all!

I had thought of everything; I had done everything. I had set my alarm and woken up hours earlier to be ready on time and to make it all appear effortless, natural. I had prepared Ashley's church bag with diapers, wipes, binkies, and snacks. I had bathed her, changed her, fed her, and dressed her. I had planned her outfit, slipped on her matching lace-trimmed socks, buttoned her tiny, impossibly soft Italian leather Mary Janes.

And then I had wrapped her up, sweet smelling and smiling, and handed her to Billy. As a gesture, a moment. As a way to pretend that we were a family. I just needed him to hold her. "Please just hold our baby for two minutes, Billy, so that I can have a free hand to put on my lipstick and gather my purse." *If putting her safely on the bed had been an option, I would've put her on the bed myself. I wanted to partner with you, involve you, parent with you, rely on you, trust you. I wanted having a baby with you to change everything about you and our relationship.*

I knew deep down in my bones that he would probably mess it up, but how can you mess up holding a baby? Exactly the way he had just messed up, I guess. I had ignored my instincts and Ashley had gotten hurt. I had bitten my tongue and tried to pretend that he was up to the task, but he wasn't. I felt not only like I was alone, but that I was also responsible for him. And if he failed, he would take us all down with him. He was at the head of our family. He was our leader, both spiritually and temporally. The provider, the caretaker, the hero. Our future was dependent on his success in every single arena. My quality of life and that of my children depended on his ability to achieve. If his train jumped the tracks, we'd tumble down right beside him. And if I couldn't trust him to hold a baby, how could I trust him to make sure my dreams came true?

Ashley's cries were not abating, and she held her arm tense and rigid by her side. Something was definitely wrong.

"I think she dislocated her shoulder," I offered with absolute confidence. I had no idea what a shoulder dislocation looked like nor did I have any experience with anything orthopedic, but it sounded like that might be what happened, and it made me feel better to diagnose her. "She's not moving her arm and her cries are getting worse." I knelt on the floor holding my daughter to my chest, feeling abandoned and alone, as if I were on the prairie surrounded by miles of snow while the wolves circled in.

"I think we need to go to the hospital," I said in a panic when it was clear he wasn't offering any suggestions. "She's not moving her arm."

I stood up and cradled her gently. I looked at her face twisted in pain and confusion, and my own sobs came forth and began to match hers in intensity and volume. I couldn't keep it together. I wanted to scream. I wanted to rip my clothes and throw a lamp through a window. I was scared, sad, and sick of pretending that Billy was enough. I could not count on him for *anything*, but I was supposed to count on him for *everything*.

I wanted to scream: "Do you know why she's never fallen off a bed before? Because I'VE NEVER PUT HER DOWN ON ONE. HELP ME. HELP ME!"

But I didn't. I didn't say any of those things. Instead, I just sat there and cried without words and let my tears blend with the tears of my firstborn—*rain-soaked and voice choked like silent screaming in a dream.*

Once we got in the car, I wanted to hold Ashley on my lap. She was blue from crying, and the thought of moving her tiny broken arm to fit into the seat belt restraints was too much to handle. I placed her in the car seat, but I kept her swaddled and only buckled the main belt across her waist. Billy watched my every move in the rearview mirror.

"You have to take the blanket off and pull her arms through the straps," he said.

I stiffened at his instruction. "The hospital is only three miles away—we'll be fine. Just drive," I pleaded. But Billy wouldn't have it.

"It's not safe," he said.

Not safe? Suddenly the man who minutes earlier had balanced a baby on a precipice was now concerned about safety?

"She has to be strapped in her car seat," he proclaimed. As if he knew. As if he fucking knew anything. *Are you kidding me? Are you kidding me right now?* I was crying too hard to argue, and Ashley's wails only added to the chaos. I knew if I wanted him to drive us to the hospital, I needed to do what he said. I walked around to the back seat and gingerly removed her blanket, pulling her tiny stiff arm through the car seat strap. She arched and screamed.

"I CAN'T DO IT, BILLY! HER ARM IS BROKEN."

I let the intensity of the moment justify the chance to scream at him—to let it out—and it felt so good. It felt like I was in *The Green Mile* letting out a thousand black flies of resentment and rage.

"SHE'S IN PAIN! I DON'T KNOW WHAT TO DO."

This is your fault. You put her down. You need to fix it.

"She will be in a lot more pain if we get in an accident," he said condescendingly.

He was not my partner; he was my liability. And yet, despite it all, he was still in charge.

Ashley cried the entire way to the hospital, and my sobs matched hers decibel for decibel. There were so many things I wanted to say, so many feelings I wanted to set free, but I said nothing. I cried and cried my broken, jaded heart out. I had choked down a thousand sobs like this before, and now I was finally letting it all out. Even when I'd thought of everything, Billy could still sabotage things whether he meant to or not.

We sat in the waiting room at St. Mark's Hospital and ranked our injuries with those of the other patients. Ashley's cries were beginning to quiet down, but mine weren't stopping. The triage nurse asked us the specifics of her accident, sizing up the credibility of our story with each notation on the clipboard. The waiting room was filling up with patients. Mostly adults, cradling various wounds and body parts. We were the only ones there in full Sunday dress, holding a screaming baby. I felt confident that we'd get moved to the top of the list and see a doctor immediately. The only patient who seemed worse off than us was an elderly woman dragging around a dirty bath towel to soak up the blood from a nosebleed.

Despite our circumstances, it still took almost two hours before we were seen by the pediatric specialist. By then, Ashley had stopped crying and had fallen asleep exhausted in my arms. My own cries had been replaced with a white-hot resentment for the wasted day, the wasted tears, and what I feared was going to be a wasted life.

A few X-rays and ibuprofen doses later, we headed back home. Our baby's arm was not broken, just banged up. Her face had a tiny abrasion, but no permanent damage. The doctors believed that it had been an unfortunate accident, and not the result of child neglect or bad parenting. In my eyes, they were dead wrong. But it wasn't Billy who was the bad parent, it was me. I was the only one guilty of child neglect, rolling the dice with her safety out of my own need to feel supported. The doctors predicted a full recovery for Ashley without calling Child Protective Services and wished us well.

They did not notice or attempt to diagnose what had broken inside of me that day. The prognosis for my future would have been much more grim.

The drive home from the hospital was dark. Billy seemed happy and back to baseline, but I was feeling the burden of the world on my shoulders. I loved this little girl. It was my job to keep her safe, and the delusion that I was doing it with an equal partner was now gone. I had tried that, and she had gotten hurt. I would have to be vigilant. If I let up on my grip for even a second, if I yielded to him, deferred to his needs over hers in even the smallest way, Ashley's future would be compromised.

I would have to reprogram my brain, restructure the way I had previously imagined motherhood and parenting and the fantasies and pictures I had stored up in my mind. When I had previously thought about being a mom, it was always in the context of being a wife first. I wanted to be a good mom to prove my value as a woman and as a wife. I wanted to be a good return on the investment that Billy had made. I believed back then that part of being a good mom and a good wife meant training my husband to be a good father. It was my job to make sure that he was involved and engaged with the children in meaningful ways that encouraged him to participate but didn't overwhelm him with too much responsibility.

That afternoon, as we left the emergency room, I was absolutely emotionally exhausted. I felt like the nosebleed bath towel our fellow patient had been dragging around the waiting room: bloodied and war-torn, desperate and heavy. The weight and shock of the last few hours surrounded me, and it was hard to make small talk on the way home. Billy seemed absolutely unaffected, jubilant, if anything, that the emergency room visit had been unremarkable, with no expensive surgeries or hospital stays. And he was pretty sure the whole incident would be covered by our insurance! Every time he tried to say something positive or chipper, I wanted to grab the back of his head by the hair and slam his face into the steering wheel. "SHUT UP. Please SHUT UP. Do you see the scrape on her face? Do you see the look of disgust on mine? Read the room."

I wasn't just getting over the drama of the day; I was actively decon-structing my entire belief structure surrounding marriage and family and gender roles. I wasn't up for small talk. I was figuring out what to do because I knew I was fucked. And I couldn't deny it any longer. I didn't want to raise kids with Billy, but thre was no way out. Divorce hadn't been an option for me in the first year of our marriage when our incompatibility became embarrassingly obvious. When I had suggested divorce to my mom, she scoffed and told me to figure out a way to make the marriage work: "We don't get divorced in our family." And that was the attitude *before* we had kids. Before we had irretrievably commingled both funds and genetics. We had a baby now, so we were bound to each other forever regardless of the status of our marriage. I couldn't leave him, I couldn't train him, and I couldn't envision how to do it alone.

The same cloud of dark emptiness that had first appeared during the sunrise over the Haleakala Crater began to creep back in. My illusions of family life were imploding just like they had on my honeymoon. *You're on your own, kid; you always have been.* I would have to scratch the original plan and start constructing a new one. I'd have to stop wasting energy on encouraging and training my husband and instead channel it into covering up and overcompensating for what we lacked: "He's the cutest dad." "He always gets a little pouty face when he gets home from work and realizes the kids are already in bed." I told these little lies to myself and to my friends and to my family even though I didn't believe them, because I finally realized that doing everything means lying about it too.

FOURTEEN

DIVORCE CAMP

Partners!! Feeling trapped in an unequal relationship? Has your sense of self and independence been completely lost and forsaken? Have we got the solution for you! As a result of innumerable complaints seeking guidance in marriages that have failed to live up to the falsified and fantastical expectations promised therein, we, the firm of Independent Ingénues, have decided to offer a new, groundbreaking, innovative, foolproof solution for all people seeking to reclaim their time, energy, power, and autonomy. It's as simple as one word, two syllables, and three vowels: DIVORCE.

For the mere cost of your spouse, your good standing in the community, and the ambiguous fee of a family lawyer, you too can trade in the shackles of a selfless marriage for a life of uncomplicated freedom. Really! It's that simple.

Do you feel your soul dying a little more each day? Do you find yourself dreading the sound of your partner speaking, chewing, breathing? Then DIVORCE is for you. It's exhausting to explain where to find the scissors and to constantly have to remind someone when an important birthday is approaching. You shouldn't have to sit through another bad retelling of the same tired anecdote or listen to their hours-long musings on topics of little to no value. When you express your feelings, hobbies, or interests, you should have the full attention of your spouse, but if they interrupt, gaslight, name-call ("hysterical" or "emotional"), or just completely ignore you, then DIVORCE may be exactly what you're looking for. If your partner doesn't think you know how to read a map, or if they explain everything to you in a baby-like cadence, just file for DIVORCE and you'll never have to listen to their annoying voice ever again.

Do you feel completely exhausted by the routine and rituals of married life? Tired of cooking and cleaning for two with little help or support from your spouse? Consider DIVORCE. Being married is really draining, and it's unfair that almost all of your work goes undermined or unnoticed by your spouse. The truth is, it's inevitable that one of you has gotten the ick by now. An ick you never could've foreseen during your first years of wedded life. But now that you've gotten it, it's impossible to undo. You shouldn't have to be chained to the ICK forever. FREE YOURSELF! It's not your responsibility to parent another adult. If you want to quit but feel trapped, just know that DIVORCE is a simple and viable option perfect for a hardworking individual like yourself.

Does the thought of waking up next to your partner every morning send a bone-rattling chill down your spine? Is their morning breath becoming increasingly worse? Is the random fart in their sleep no longer charming? DIVORCE is your answer. Don't feel compelled to spend another night tossing and turning because your spouse's cold foot has drifted onto your side and bumped up against your leg. You can enjoy eight hours of blissful rest without hearing chortled snores and staggered breaths. Just kick them *out of bed and get a DIVORCE. You'll never have to wake up groggy again, and all of your cozy dreams will be free to continue uninterrupted. Sleep tight knowing that your future is uninhibited by the whims of a person with an erratic libido. There's no need to get used to the incessant whir of a CPAP machine or the sight of a slobbery retainer on the nightstand; enjoy nights of soundless slumber. Enjoy an environment free of dirty Q-tips and used dental floss with DIVORCE!*

Do you shudder at the prospect of spending Friday night watching yet another movie not of your choosing, grow frustrated with the thought of sacrificing your last bowl of sacred Cocoa Puffs, or cower at the idea of a weekend with your mother-in-law? Look no further than DIVORCE. Take back your life and reclaim your free time. Feel like you can enjoy the simple things that made you happy as a single person once again. Indulge in nights of binge-watching Netflix with a carton of Ben and Jerry's knowing, with confidence, that no one else's spoon tracks will have left nothing but a bite at the bottom.

Is toothpaste spit dirtying the sink? A stray pubic hair on the toilet seat staring back at you? For both complaints, DIVORCE provides a simple solution. Have the bathroom all to yourself, and never feel threatened by the messy, dirty, haphazard presence of another person in your home. Hang a bouquet of aloe from your showerhead, install new lights above your mirror, leave your skin care products in a place of easy access without fear of question or ridicule, and enjoy the peace and serenity of a partner-free life with DIVORCE.

Watch as confidence and freedom come back ever so gradually. You too can be an independent person once again, no matter how blinded and suffocated you feel in the depths of marriage.

Hurry and file! Don't let another day go by where you are subjected to their views and are forced to acknowledge their presence. DIVORCE is the solution to every marital burden. Isn't it about time you were in complete control? Reclaim the identity you deserve.

So, what are you waiting for? You want to lose 150 pounds overnight? File for DIVORCE and get rid of all that dead weight. Call now. Spots are unlimited.

FIFTEEN

THE E IS IMPORTANT

On the streets of Park City, Hollywood comes to Utah. Sundance is one of the prime-time opportunities for wannabe Good-Time Girls to get their game on.

The Sundance Film Festival arrives in Utah once a year in late January, and for a landlocked town of repressed Mormons, it can be the one and only annual glimpse into a life of glamor, glitz, and gluttony. Park City is a mountain resort town forty-five minutes outside of Salt Lake City and is an oasis carved away from the chokehold of conservative values, stringent liquor laws, curfews, and police-state morality that plagues almost every other city in the state.

During the mining era, Park City was referred to as Sin City because it was the only place in Utah where you could buy 5-percent-alcohol beer or malt beverages in the local convenience stores. Everywhere else, you were restricted to state-run liquor stores that didn't open until 11:00 a.m. and closed at 9:00 p.m. during the week. These liquor stores are still the only places that sell wines and spirits in the entire state of Utah. They are closed on Sundays and on holidays. This means that, in the year of our Lord 2024, if you don't buy your champagne by 4:00 p.m. on the afternoon before Easter, there will be no mimosas at brunch, and you'll be forced to raise a flat, leftover White Claw to celebrate the resurrection of our Lord. That level of shame and scarcity is exactly what the church leaders had in mind when they instituted the liquor laws that govern our beloved Beehive State.

The strict liquor laws aren't any more or less absurd than many of the self-imposed requirements followed by members of the Church of Jesus Christ of Latter-Day Saints. In fact, most members are blissfully unaware of the liquor laws because they simply don't apply to them and are therefore irrelevant. But for the rest of the population, it can feel quite oppressive to have your drunken binges limited to post office hours. If you want a nightcap at 10:30 p.m., you'd better hit the liquor store before they shutter for the night or your only option will be the 3-percent beer and hard seltzers available in a locked refrigerator case behind a curtain at appropriately zoned 7-Eleven stores.

You have to understand the thumb we are typically under in order to understand what a *gift* the Sundance Festival feels like. It is a wrinkle in time, a magical passageway into the world of the Hollywood elite, a chance for the country mice to experience a taste of big-city life right in their own backyard.

I myself experienced Sundance for the first time when I was a coed at BYU. I was nineteen and college-life broke, but rich with naiveté and ambition. My friends and I dreamed of going to Park City and using our righteous glow and innocence to slip behind the elusive red-velvet rope right into an after-hours party and the arms of a famous director,

Me. Denver, Colorado. 1980s.

My dad and family while white-water rafting. Green River, Utah. 1994.

Twelve women on a beach. Newport Beach, California. 1992.

Me and Guillermo. Tijuana, Mexico. 1992.

Martha Bourne. Salt Lake City, Utah. 1992.

Me at Brigham Young University. Provo, Utah. 1993.

Me on my mission handing a Catholic statue the Book of Mormon. Marseille, France. 1998.

Me and Billy right before I was pushed inside the limo. Laie, Hawaii. 2000.

Me and Billy on our honeymoon. Maui, Hawaii. 2000.

Me and Snoop Dogg. Salt Lake City, Utah. 2015.

Me and Grey. Salt Lake City, Utah. 2021.

Me at the *Bad Mormon* cover shoot. Burbank, California. 2021.

Me and my crew at The Abbey. West Hollywood, California. 2021.

Four women on a beach. Bermuda. 2023. Courtesy of Bravo.

Me and the Salt Lake City Housewives. Salt Lake City, Utah. 2023.

Me and Angie Katsanevas.
Salt Lake City, 2024.

Me and my daughters. Maui, Hawaii. 2023.

actor, or even cameraman. It didn't matter who it was as long as he was wearing an All-Access Pass on a retractable lanyard. Bonus points were granted if he knew how to order drinks for underage girls willing to do anything—as long as it didn't compromise our hymens, our college education, or our parents' expectations. We were bound by the BYU Honor Code, but only until we crossed county lines. If we were caught doing something against the Honor Code in Park City—or anywhere else for that matter—we would still get expelled. But at Sundance, Provo, Utah, felt a million miles away, and we were emboldened by the distance. In the wild frontier, we were free to go full Hollywood, baby. Oh how the mice will play when the cat's away!

At least that was the idea we'd cooked up in our heads. The reality of Sundance was much colder, more chaotic, and more eye-opening than I'd expected. "Going to Sundance" when you have no money, no connections, and no outstanding genetics is a parade of rejection up and down Main Street, with security guards for hire standing under heat lamps shooing you away before you can even remove your mittens to look for your fake ID.

I had taken my older sister Jenny's expired driver's license that she had foolishly discarded when she got married at nineteen and taken on her husband's name. She was five years older and only vaguely resembled me, but with a beanie, scarf, and added parka, I hoped to sneak through the chaos at the door with my overwhelming charm.

It never happened . . . The closest we got to any Hollywood parties was a dive bar that, for lack of patrons, reluctantly let us in in an effort to appear as populated as the corporate-sponsored venues that flanked and outranked them on either side.

We stripped off our layers of outerwear to reveal our meticulously planned outfits for the evening. I was wearing a little number that still ranks in the top five of my most favorite outfits of all time. It was a matching set—two distinct but coordinated pieces—that I had saved and sacrificed for in order to purchase from my favorite store: Express. It was an A-line black suede miniskirt with white contrast stitching that snapped up the front, with a matching vest. The fabric was stiff and unbrushable, and when I took the skirt off, it stood on its own like a black lampshade in the middle of my room. I wanted to look as sexy as possible in order to increase my chances of being discovered, so I paired it with a thick white turtleneck, thick black tights, and my all-weather snow boots. It was an outfit that would never be allowed on campus at BYU. My fellow students would have reported me to the Honor Code Office if I dared show up to class dressed so sluttily. The Honor Code was very specific about skirt lengths and sleeves. Clothing had to be knee length and tank tops and sleeveless shirts were forbidden. Tight clothing was easier to get away with, but eventually, leggings grew to be discouraged entirely. If you showed up at the testing center in a pair of lululemons, you'd be denied access. I was violating laws with both length and snugness. The skirt stopped at least two inches above my knee, and in these frigid temperatures, if I unsnapped the vest and stuck my chest out, eagle-eyed passersby might have been lucky enough to see the outline of a frozen nipple. In my mind, I was the hottest ingénue to hit Sundance, both figuratively and with my many insulated layers, quite literally.

My friend and I wanted to look like seasoned regulars, so we busied ourselves by pretending to play a game of pool, flirting with whomever looked halfway in our direction, and praying that they were transplants from the Golden State or the Big Apple and not just locals with the same thirsty agenda as us. And then . . . we saw him: a real, live Hollywood actor from a real, live television show: *Beverly Hills, 90210*. It wasn't Jason Priestley or Ian Ziering or *gasp* . . . Luke Perry. It was a deep cut. A side character that had fulfilled a mini-arc as John, the dark fraternity brother nemesis of Ziering's character, Steve. He was our ticket: not famous enough to dismiss us out of hand, but famous enough to be an anecdote that we could dine out on for the rest of our lives.

His entourage was small, and despite his good looks and film credits, he, even in a local bar, did not carry himself with main-character energy. He knew what it felt like to be second fiddle to the big stars in the room and we as good Christian women knew that feeling all too well. Snaring him was within our grasp. We started out subtly making eye contact and nudging each other. Then we gave in, rushed over, and obnoxiously asked him, "Are you on TV?" We held our breath, anticipating his response. Our enthusiasm was so effusive that he was unable to just brush us off. He even cracked a smile. He flipped his long bangs back and said: "Yeah, I am. That's me. I'm the guy that got kicked out of the fraternity for date rape. It sucks, because now I don't really know if they're going to be able to bring me back."

Beverly Hills, 90210 had aired an episode where a date rapist was subjected to a ritual called "blackballing." Blackballing is when the fraternity brothers hold either a white or black ball and then, at a designated time and all at once, reveal their ball in a dramatic ceremony. A white ball signifies acceptance of a fraternity brother. A black ball represents rejection. Steve led the charge. He informed everyone of

John's predatory ways and campaigned against him, despite their prior friendship. Turning his back on his brothers for the girls . . . he was basically a knight in Girbaud jeans and a rugby.

But here in the halls of Sundance, this reputation as a date rapist made the actor who'd played John all the more alluring! He was a side character we remembered, an actual significant episode marked in time that we could refer to when we later shared our thirsty Sundance stories with the inhabitants of the parched land that was BYU.

His entourage was small and eclectic and made up entirely of men. A band of Hollywood brothers, we mused, and we clung to them like Disney side characters. The boys assumed we were drunk. Only an intoxicated person would have the confidence and bravado we displayed, but we were stone sober. When they asked casually if we wanted to "get out of here," we readily agreed, not considering what that actually implied. As we gathered up our belongings and made one last lap of the still pretty empty bar, I found myself alone in a dark corridor by the bathroom with a member of Black Ball's entourage. The confined space forced us closer than I would have dared otherwise, and feeling flirtatious and free, I leaned in . . . and was met with a hearty response.

Before I could even fully prepare myself for this impetuous kiss, Black Ball's friend of a friend flipped me around, pressed me up against the wall, and forced his knee between my legs. I gasped in fear and excitement, but mostly fear, as he took his hand and shoved it up the back of my skirt, pulling down my tights just below my butt. I felt protests pound my brain. What was happening? We hadn't even kissed yet! This didn't feel like assault; it felt like a normal rite of passage. However, it was a rite of passage I hadn't yet experienced, so I had nothing to compare it to. After all, I had begged for this. Why wear so many layers if you didn't want someone to desperately rip them off?

As he pinned me against the wall, he growled in my ear, "You just want to fuck me so bad, don't you?"

Wait a minute, "fuck"? Do you mean "do it"? Like, tonight? Aren't we skipping a lot of steps here? Do we have time for you to pack a romantic picnic, meet my dad, and hear all of my hopes and fears? It's practically 10 p.m. already!

Every vision I had of my future flashed across my eyes: my hope chest, my white wedding in a white temple, my future husband with grateful tears in his eyes that I had saved myself for him and him alone. Everything I believed in hung in the balance. I *did* want to fuck him so bad—even more than my professor Alan Smithson—but I wanted the dream and promise of the future I'd been planning on more. I panicked.

The question pierced through all of my naive fantasies. I realized that, even if he was saying what I secretly wanted, it was also what I secretly feared, and it broke the delusion entirely.

I squirmed out of his grasp, pulled my tights up and my skirt down, and bolted from the hallway into the bar. I grabbed my friend's arm dramatically and opened my eyes wide with fear and in warning: "We can't go with them. Just trust me. We can't."

We squeezed past the drunk bar patrons up the stairs to Main Street, and started running as fast as we could toward our parked car. I was escaping, running from myself and from the mysterious dark world that I found so alluring.

We loaded into the car and headed for the highway. Driving home to Happy Valley and the safety of our supervised campus housing felt like both victory and defeat.

Nearly twenty years later, after my divorce, I found myself trekking back up the canyon toward Sundance yet again. I was newly single and my husband had moved out and moved on, but I was still *very* Mormon and a mom of three. I had, however, maintained the same thirst for danger and lust for blackballed groupies. The girl I had been in the black suede matching set still burned bright within my bosom.

Again, I planned my outfit meticulously. Black on black on black on black on boots. But this time around, I ditched the turtleneck and added a push-up bra and fur vest for flair. I was no longer a teen with a fake ID. Now, the security guys baking under heat lamps would be able to tell immediately that I was of age, and they probably wouldn't even ask me to crack my wallet. It was my moment for a do-over. I had money now, I had worldly friends, and more importantly, I had experience. I could fuck someone *so bad* if I really wanted to.

This time, I wasn't looking for Hollywood . . . I was just looking for anybody. I was in what I affectionately like to call the "whore phase" of my divorce. The "whore phase" is a cherished window of time when you have a voracious appetite to be held, to be loved, to be manhandled.

We had friends working the door at Park City Live, so we knew we could get in and we knew we could get a table. And once you have a table in a crowded club, you can pretty much meet anyone you want. On a busy night during Sundance, people will gladly sell their body, soul, and a six-month situationship for the chance to sit down at a table inside, free from the throng of wet down coats mixed with sweat, need, and an unquenchable thirst for the spotlight.

Estevan stood out among the guys because he was exceptionally striking. He had what I can only describe as a European haircut AND a scarf. And not a scarf for warmth in winter, but a decorative scarf for flair. When he walked up and introduced himself, I could've sworn I heard an accent and I melted in place. He didn't have an actual accent, mind you, but just his foreign name was enough to make me hear one.

I asked him where he was from with a fancy name like Estevan, and he told me his family was from Argentina. He said he was a professional fitness model, so I told him that I was a professional photographer specializing in fitness models! I was padding my resumé a bit, but I didn't see any harm in a little white lie. It was a small price to pay.

I didn't even need to bribe him with free headshots. He took my hand and led me to my car in the multilevel parking structure. We got in and immediately turned the heat up. We reclined our seats, and I put on music while he put on the moves. We talked and laughed and kissed for hours. It was the exact opposite of my hallway fling from twenty years before. There was no hand up the skirt or whispered desires, just middle-aged window fogging.

Estevan's phone kept ringing and ringing and ringing, and he would just decline the call every single time. At one point, I came up for air and said, "Shouldn't you answer that?" But he shrugged off the suggestion. I never once considered that it might be a concerned wife, an angry girlfriend, an emergency, or a red flag because . . . it didn't matter. I was living in my own fantasy about who he was and why we needed each other. I imagined him as a lonely Argentinian transplant, thrust into the harsh world of modeling, left all alone, deprived of carbohydrates, and forced to maintain 4 percent body fat while managing a demanding life of open calls and runway rejections. I would be his soft place to land: a well-insulated pillow on which my dear Estevan could rest his weary, chiseled face each and every night.

He would sing me songs from the old country like "(Stand Back) Buenos Aires," and I would dream of trips to Rio de Janeiro, frustrating him when I failed to understand the difference between Argentina and Brazil, much less the difference between Portuguese and Spanish. We would franchise our own Empanada Mama and travel the world with passports from different countries to visit friends near and far. Everything I liked about him was based on the idea that he was from a different country and also a model. So long as I kept him within the preconceptions of my own imagination, we could stay together forever.

When security made their final rounds and evicted us from the parking garage, we made plans to meet again "for a photo shoot," but I had no intention of bringing my camera. My plan worked. We started hooking up, and I began planning "photo shoots" weekly. After all, it's very important for a young model to build his portfolio. Our trysts were the closest thing to having a forbidden lover that I had ever experienced, but I told myself and anyone else who asked that our relationship was purely professional.

After a few weeks, reality began sinking in. It became harder and harder to merge our lives. I was juggling three kids and post-divorce trauma, and he was busy doing whatever fitness models do when they aren't at work—sit-ups, calorie counting, and full body shaving. We mostly met at his condo after hours whenever I could sneak away and we rarely went out in public.

Our love affair ended abruptly the one night we decided to take it public. We were at a sushi bar in downtown SLC sharing a volcano roll.

A mutual friend walked in and was astonished to see us together. He exclaimed, "Hey, Heather! I didn't know you knew Steve."

I didn't know I knew Steve either. "Who the fuck is *Steve?*" I asked. "This is ESTEVAN."

My friend looked just as confused as I was: "Who is *Estevan?*" he asked. "This is STEVE."

Apparently I was on a date with Steve, *not* Estevan, a familiar face around the local Planet Fitness where he worked as a front desk receptionist—aka a fitness model, as in hand me a towel and model the appropriate use of the fitness equipment. Turns out, *Steve* had recently decided to turn his life around, which precipitated a name change in honor of his Argentinian heritage. He was going to introduce himself to people he met from here on out as "Estevan," and he was going to say he was a "fitness model" rather than a purple-polo-wearing front desk attendant at the gym. All of a sudden, my Argentinian model Estevan became a totally average guy from Pleasant Grove named Steve. In his mind, offering me the world meant offering me a complimentary membership to Planet Fitness. Estevan was not from Buenos Aires. He was from a suburb in Utah County where there's not even a Empanada Mama within a hundred-mile radius.

I was willing to offer my services to an up-and-coming Argentinian model named Estevan, but my generosity did not extend to the staff or Steves of Planet Fitness. I stopped offering free photo sessions, and Steve didn't even put up a fight. He was used to rejection, and our photo shoots were taking away precious time that could be spent rounding out his biceps. Once I was forced to face the truth of who he was, it suddenly revealed an even uglier truth: who I was, and what I was willing to settle for.

What's in a name? I'll tell you: *fucking* everything. Steve née Estevan had clearly seen plenty of Anthony Robbins self-help videos and had decided on a name- and career-change pivot. You can call yourself whatever you want at Planet Fitness, but this relationship was certainly not a Judgement Free Zone®.

Turns out that the E in Estevan is important. If you take it away, you're left with Steven . . . or still worse, Steve. And who *really* wants to date a "Steve"? For the first time since we'd locked eyes across the room in that sweaty bar in Park City, the hard reality of our situation sunk in. I finally admitted to myself the cold hard truth, *Estevan and I are not meant to be. In no part of the world, no universe could a Heather ever love a Steve.*

SIXTEEN

THUNDER THIGHS

want to be sex positive. I really do . . . and I want to have great sex, frequently. But I also do not want to keep making the compromises that great sex seems to require.

The importance of compromise becomes glaringly obvious in my conversations with friends who are in this same dilemma. When it comes to dating later in life, we are often caught between a rock and a sometimes *not so* hard place. It's all fun and games until you find yourself announcing at brunch, "I just slept with a landscaper that I thought would rock my world, but instead he ended up apologizing for his intermittent erections and revealed that he was recovering from a recent tummy tuck." I don't want to sleep with a guy getting the same plastic surgery as me. And your ever-enabling friends immediately pipe in with soothing responses: "Well, that doesn't sound too bad. Imagine what it would've been like without the tummy tuck."

This is what dating has come to for me and my kind. This is dating post-divorce. This is dating in your forties and beyond—post child-rearing, post career-making, post promises of weddings and bridesmaids and picket fences and grandchildren. This era of dating is barren and logistical. It's a land where all the normal trappings of love seem to be irrelevant.

"Is he tall?" Does it matter? I'm not concerned about passing on his genetics.

"Is he employed?" Does it matter? I have enough income for both of us.

If you have no desire to ever get married again or have more children, the potential titles of "Good Husband" and "Good Father" are both theoretically irrelevant. But, who really wants to hang out with a deadbeat dad? And, if you're a good person, aren't you naturally a "Good Husband" and "Good Father"?

Another big deal breaker to drop off my list was "Good Provider." Now that I can provide for myself, my family, and then some, factoring in my partner's ability to buy me things is, again, irrelevant. But does irrelevance also signify that it's unimportant? After all, who wants to date a deadbeat employee? And, if you're smart and passionate and hardworking, aren't you naturally gainfully employed, ambitious, and a "Good Provider"?

When I was twenty years old and dating to get married, my list of deal breakers was as long and thorough as an iPhone's terms and conditions. And yet I still ended up getting divorced. Now when I consider dating someone, the deal breakers are far less rigorous. They're more like a BuzzFeed quiz: "Which breakfast item do you prefer?"

When kids and genetics and family values are no longer relevant, what are the criteria on which you can build a relationship? You can call yourself open-minded, but the second you walk into a house with paneled canvas prints of old-timey saloon ladies from the reduced bin of T.J.Maxx, you realize pretty quickly that any relations from that point on will require a compromise. Are you willing to sleep with a guy who breeds dachshunds but only refers to them as "wiener dogs"? Are you willing to sleep with a guy who decorates his mantel with a row of beer steins from Harry Potter's Collector Cup series? Nothing great comes without sacrifice, and it's up to you to decide whether or not membership in a Pokémon Facebook group is a fair trade-off for being manhandled by a lumberjack with thunder thighs. And in my opinion, it's sixes.

Everyone knows that if you want to have ugly sex, it's easier to do it with the lights off. And by ugly sex, I mean sex with someone who isn't pretty . . . on paper or in real life. But dating now seems like ugly sex all the time, and it's not only easier with the lights off, it's necessary. I'm not talking about physical lights here. You have to turn the lights off in your brain. You have to achieve a total, complete, pitch-black lack of awareness in order to face yourself in the mirror the morning after.

Are you willing to date a guy who breathes on your vagina during oral sex? Like it's an add-on service? It doesn't even matter if it feels good, because you can't get over the visual of him selecting the hot wax special at the automated car wash and thinking to himself, *Oh yeah, she's getting the upgrade!*

Are you willing to adapt to the smell and taste of Listerine? Not minty modern Listerine, but yellow, fuel-burning, old-school medicinal Listerine? Even if the guy who gargles with it has a vacation home in Aspen? I mean, I was . . . only to learn that the Listerine smell traveled with him. And once that scent is burned into your nostrils, it's hard to ever forget. I can't use Listerine to this day; I have to use Crest Fresh Mint with fluoride.

Then there are the red flags you're willing to overlook. "Yes, of course I can see that he has four other girls' names tattooed on his arm, but who doesn't have a past these days?" "Okay, sure . . . so it's a little weird that all his paychecks are garnished to cover his child support, but at least he *has* a paycheck!" The trade-offs are endless, and I don't know if I've gotten more desperate or just less precious about who I mess around with.

Immediately after my separation, dating was easy . . . so easy that I've been trying to hack the system and reverse engineer it so I can figure out why it's so much more difficult these days. I don't know if it is because back then my potential partners and I were all younger and sexier and yearning for more of an escape, or if it is because I was more wounded, more self-destructive, and ravenous for acceptance in whatever form it manifested. But no matter the reason, ten years later, the landscape seems drastically altered. Everyone has moved on to second marriages or second divorces. I no longer need an excuse to get out of the house to escape chores or children. My kids are self-sufficient, I outsource every chore and meal I can, and Instacart brings me taro tea *and* chlorine tabs for the swimming pool. I want for *nothing*. My house has become my kingdom, over which I preside with complacent and comfortable reign.

I figured that once I got famous, the dating landscape would change and I'd have more opportunities to meet more fantastic men. But if anything, fame has made it harder to put myself out there. Everything feels loaded with potential problems: stumbling through relationships with two left feet isn't something I want to do with the whole world watching. And it's not just my actions I'm worried about, but my potential boyfriend's too. Sabrina Carpenter said it best in "Please Please Please": "Heartbreak is one thing, my ego's another / I beg you don't embarrass me, motherfucker."

I'm still caught up in the programming that the only type of sex that isn't shameful is sex between committed married partners. A lot of my sexual bravado on television or in conversation is just born out of comedy at best, projection at worst. I don't have a ton of sexual experience, mostly because I started so late and I started out in absolute secrecy. I don't think I'd feel comfortable introducing a "boyfriend" to anyone in my family. A fiancé, maybe, but I still feel conspicuous about having sex outside of marriage. Outside of commitment. Because I'm the only single girl in my group of friends, in real life and on television, somehow my sex life has become public domain, and I have played into it.

Like I said, I want to be sex positive, I really do, but I feel a lot of shame for still being single. It's especially uncomfortable to talk about my sex life when I'm surrounded by my married friends. It's like they all have name-brand bags and I'm carrying a knockoff.

I don't know why talking about sex at this point in my life makes me so uncomfortable. I'd rather use euphemism and conjecture than accurate terms, and I'd rather close my eyes to the realities than talk about it honestly. Dating or talking about dating for me now requires the lights off. In my head and in my heart. Maybe that's why ugly sex, when it comes down to it, is the most appealing of all. And if that's the case, I'm just getting started.

SEVENTEEN

WEST HOLLYWOOD

I went through the Church of Jesus Christ of Latter-day Saints temple endowment ceremony for the very first time on October 26. This was the day that I received the saving ordinances for myself and received my new, awful-sounding, sacred temple name. The ritual began with women circling me, blessing me, and preparing me for adulthood and womanhood as a righteous daughter of God—a Good Mormon, if you will.

Decades later, on another October 26, I found myself similarly surrounded by women. This time, however, I was in a studio in Burbank, California, in front of a lighted mirror with glam professionals blessing me with foundation and contour and hair extensions, preparing me not for marriage, but for a portrait as an apostate—a woman who had turned her back on her faith. It was a photo shoot for the cover of my first book: a memoir about my life, which marked a great departure from the devout, rule-abiding woman who stood in the temple for the first time on that same date years before. I was now, as the title of my book declared, a *Bad Mormon*.

I was really doing it. I was leaving the church and declaring it in the most public way possible. An act that, for years, I never could have imagined. When I was a believing member, I never doubted that my faith would ebb and flow. I was sure there would be times in my life when my belief might dwindle, but I never once questioned my commitment to the cause. I thought I'd always be Mormon. It was the most central part of my identity. Yet here I was, ripping the Band-Aid off and setting myself up in opposition to the church and culture that I had identified with since birth. It is one thing to quietly quit the church while still going through the motions. It is another thing to quit and quietly admit it to your closest friends and family. But it is an *entirely* different and *bigger* thing to announce that you are leaving, to write a book about leaving, and to talk about the secrets that you promised never to divulge. The book, *Bad Mormon*—its contents, its title, and its cover with my name and likeness—would be a slap in the face to my family and some of my closest friends. It was treacherous on many levels. Like Jean Valjean in *Les Miserables*, I was not only betraying my benefactor, I was also stealing the silverware on my way out the door.

I was scared—petrified even—to publish the book. In my initial meeting for the cover shoot, the creative director threw out the idea of me leaping in the air, full Russian splits, with a *Book of Mormon* in one hand and a glass of wine in the other—a play off the promotional materials for the massive Broadway hit *The Book of Mormon*. I hadn't jumped on a trampoline in years and even then I could never do a split, much less the Russian splits. I was also still quite new to holding a wineglass, so I was a little unsure how to appropriately hold one while leaping on a trampoline. I imagined the final cover he described: me leaping with a strained expression midair, splashing wine on the only outfit that fit while my legs splayed outward in a modified jumping jack.

When I consulted my friends about what type of book cover they envisioned, their responses horrified me: "I can see you in a messy kitchen with an apron on, hair in a bun on top of your head, and pancake batter on your cheek. Like a full-on exasperated mom screaming, 'I cook it, you clean it!'" Another friend offered a scene with me angry and enraged, tearing open an elaborately wrapped gift and discovering that the box was empty. Did my friends even know me at all? Who did they think I was, and what did they think this book was about?

The only book cover I could ever imagine for myself didn't include my image at all, much less my image as an exasperated housewife. I just wanted word art in a bold typeface with no serifs. Simple, clean: a title and an author.

I had no idea how to represent on the outside what the book signified on the inside. I wasn't sure what the right cover was going to look like, but I definitely knew that there could be no leaping, no pancake batter, no expressions of rage. And if we had to use my face, it would have to be retouched to the point where I could hardly recognize myself.

Growing up, we were surrounded by sermons and lessons on the importance of the phrase "Return with Honor." It was initially a motto ingrained in every new missionary before they embarked on their volunteer service for the Lord. A lot of the families I knew had plaques on their walls that you could see as you walked out the front door displaying the phrase in etched lettering, not unlike the "Play Like a Champion Today" poster hanging in the stairwell of the Notre Dame locker room. It was a friendly reminder of the expectations on us as we left the sanctuary of our homes and stepped out into the real world.

I knew that with both the contents and title of my book, I was forfeiting my running in the "Return with Honor" race and was instead crossing the line into the Land of No Return. The book itself was a denouncement, but I didn't want the cover image to twist the knife. If I was to properly execute this task, I knew I needed backup: Mormon Backup, Pioneer Backup, Salt of the Earth Backup. The kind of support I could only count on from a select few who understood both my desire to declare my independence and my desire to soften the blow for the believers.

I asked my friend to fly out to Los Angeles and be my sentinel at the gate. She, like myself, had grown up in the church—devout, dutiful—and later divorced. She had friends and family and stepchildren who were still practicing, and she herself was raising children who were straddling the fence, similarly to my own. She also had a background in show business, with modeling for several clothing companies and a few Hallmark movies on her resumé. I was positive that out of everyone I knew, she would be the one best equipped to balance marketability with morality.

In our creative meetings, I had suggested using an old Polaroid of me and my family with all our eyes scratched out, or perhaps an image of me holding a book over my face with devil horns peeking out from above. I just wanted something that didn't have to use my face or my body. I rarely saw a picture of myself that didn't make me want to leap into traffic. I always saw every flaw from every angle, and I hated my asymmetry and bulkiness, my nose always looking too big and my eyes always looking too small. More than hating pictures of myself, I dreaded the thought of a photo shoot. Of having to stand there and exude faux confidence and attitude in front of strangers cheering me on as if I were three years old and learning to use the potty independently.

"Can't we have a cover without me on it?" I asked.

My agent and editor kindly explained that as a first-time author, I was only getting a book deal because I was recognizable from a successful TV show. In order to get people to buy the book, they would have to recognize me on the cover. Which meant, unfortunately, I would have to be on it.

So I found myself the subject of an elaborate professional photo shoot, and I was dreading every minute of it. I needed my friend to run interference in case things started to go sideways. I had a history of people-pleasing and deference, and I knew if I was asked to leap, I would never say no. If asked to attempt the splits, I didn't want to be the one to admit I couldn't. But my friend could, and she could do it in a way that was effortless, charming, and irresistible. I front-loaded her with all this information in anticipation so there would be no surprises about the specific role she was to perform. If anything, I wanted her to lean into her conservative, shame-riddled training, just to err on the side of caution. She assured me that she would be vigilant. Her goal was to keep the photo shoot respectable, reserved, reverent even, so that I could focus on smiling and keeping my Spanx from rolling down.

She flew out to meet me on set the morning of the shoot. She arrived in a full Balmain coordinated triple set: Barbie-core bright pink denim jeans, corset, and jacket. She glided directly into the room with her arms outstretched, a million-watt smile plastered across her face. "I'm here!" she cooed. As soon as I saw her, I breathed a sigh of relief. Her energy filled the room and she put everyone at ease. She quickly surveyed the progress of my hair and makeup, nodded approval, and then beelined for the clothing rack full of potential looks. She rifled through my outfit options with a flick of her hand and openly assessed her approval/disapproval of each item. She dismissed anything too cheap or too revealing immediately and then circled back, suggesting a black tuxedo: a satin lapel jacket and matching pants as a solid starting point.

Once dressed and primped and sufficiently shellacked, the photographer positioned me under the lights and in the middle of the backdrop. It required no leaping or posing, but it still felt humiliating. Everyone staring at you, assessing you, maybe even pitying you. I hated it. They asked what type of music I wanted to listen to, and I went completely blank. What type of music did they want me to listen to? I had been creating playlists since the time of mixtapes, but I had never considered what type of music would inspire a *Bad Mormon* book cover. I froze. I wanted something soothing and dark like Bruce Springsteen's "I'm on Fire" from *Live at Giants Stadium*, but instinctively I knew that wasn't "photo shoot" music. I needed something upbeat, something that the whole room could enjoy and dance to, something mainstream and relatable but also something that spoke to my soul: "The Indigo Girls?" I asked meekly. "Brandi Carlile?"

As soon as I said the names they sounded wrong. Like I had exposed my lack of experience prematurely. Now it would be an uphill battle to win any of the crew over, and they'd probably feel compelled to cheer me on even more ardently. I immediately recanted and went fully limp: "Whatever you guys want. I like everything. I can listen to anything. Whatever the group decides." I was tripping over my supplications, doing anything just to take the attention off me and put it back on getting this all over with as soon as possible.

The team put on a random mix of songs. I was warming up slowly, but they weren't getting the flow they wanted. My friend stepped in and whispered to the photographer's assistant. They read the room and adjusted, pressing play on *The Book of Mormon* musical soundtrack. Andrew Rannells's voice filled the room and instantly, I came alive.

Once the music started and the set cleared, it was just me and my tuxedo standing there in front of a photographer asking him to make me look pretty. I had no idea what the fuck to do. Where was I supposed to put my hands? My pink dream of a friend took over and became a mirror from which I could copy every move and enter into the role I needed to play.

She assumed her position directly to the left of the photographer, serpentining through different poses—hands on hips, hand perched on lateral elbow, look down, touch sides of hair, point toe, lift toe, bend knee, throw head back, fake laugh, fake shrug, fake smile, fake it all! I'm not sure if my poses mimicked hers in any recognizable way, but just having her there for me to parrot helped me take it all a little less seriously. After all, she was out here doing it all without a photographer and without a bestselling book cover on the line. She cracked jokes and kept the crew and photographer entertained.

When we finally wrapped, I felt exhausted but hopeful that we had found a pose that would end up being perfect: a secret keeper and a secret teller, an equal touch of recognizable and reverent. We thanked the crew and piled into our car to go back to the hotel. It was time to celebrate!

"Where should we go for dinner?" I asked.

"I might just book a room at the Beverly Hills Hotel so we can eat at the Palm," she offered.

"No," I protested. "I want you to stay with me. I have a room at the Mondrian."

"Heather," she said gently, "the Mondrian was cool, like, seven years ago."

Insider information like this was exactly what I was looking for. I convinced her to forgo the Palm for dinner, and we instead settled on Craig's. She agreed that with its blend of paparazzi and people pleasing, it was the perfect place for a Housewife and aspiring author to dine. She brought her suitcase up to my room and observed the queen-sized bed and closet-like bathroom that we'd be sharing.

"Let me get my own room," she insisted.

"Don't be a snob," I pushed back. "This room is great! And it's more fun if we are together. Look at our view of the roof of the Beverly Center and stop complaining."

We called my agent and his partner and told them to meet us on the roof of our hotel for pre-dinner drinks. This was my first time meeting my highly acclaimed literary agent, Steve Troha, and I had big expectations. He represented some pretty serious names—Dolly Parton, Andrew Morton, Misty Copeland, Michael Easter—even though he himself had been blessed with a less than serious name. This Steve was the real deal, not Estevan minus the E. He was an actual literary agent, not a clerk at the local Barnes & Noble.

I was looking forward to a night out on the town enmeshed with industry luminaries. I pictured him sleek and shark-like in a dark Armani suit with exquisite tailoring, drenched in a woodsy cologne, perhaps even sporting a pinky ring. He was big time, and that's what I assumed big-time agents looked like. However, when Steve showed up he was quite the opposite. He was young and fresh-faced, ruggedly handsome and accessible, like a model plucked from the pages of a department store brochure. He was not dressed in a shark-like suit, but rather in a tan wool sweater and cotton pants. His sweater wasn't couture, but it was label conscious, with L.L.Bean displayed in thick red yarn across his chest, arching over an embroidered trout. *This sucks*, I thought. I wanted Jordan Belfort, *Wolf of Wall Street*, but based on appearance, I was getting more of an Ira Glass, *This American Life* vibe. *How will anyone know he's a VIP?*

After drinks, we all piled into our car service and rode over to Craig's. The scene was pretty thin and the food was fine. But the company was magnificent! What Steve and his partner, Isaac, lacked in over-the-top couture they made up for in looks and conversation. Our little group had immediate chemistry, and we laughed our way through all of our shared courses.

The night was still young, and I wasn't going to let a trout sweater derail my big-city plans, so after dinner we all agreed on hitting the iconic West Hollywood gay bar, The Abbey. I had heard of The Abbey, but I never imagined I'd be hanging out there . . . especially not with someone wearing L.L.Bean. Steve, fully committed to his role as full-time hometown literary professional, refused to take his sweater off despite my pleadings. It only took a few minutes before I felt comfortable enough with him to give notes on his attire and express mild disappointment in his lack of flair. He stood as firm as a Virginia dogwood. The sweater stayed on. It was representative of his brand: Southern Living with a dash of Cottage Core. He was the type of agent you could rely on—one that Dolly herself could trust with a Tennessee handshake. Turns out that even in a fish sweater, a *Heather* CAN love a *Steve*.

At the club, there were wall-to-wall men, but none of them were interested in me or in women in general until a random group sat at an adjacent table. As I looked them over, I noticed what had to be the only straight guy among them. It shouldn't have been so obvious to my untrained eye, but there he was, and I could tell that he felt as outnumbered as I did.

Ladies and Gentlemen, we have a candidate.

The night was still young, and I wanted to celebrate my book and my departure from the church with a fitting climax. I smiled, and he walked over and introduced himself as Jake.

Within minutes, he was sitting next to me at our table. And it was all happening. He joined our entourage wordlessly, and we drank and danced the night away. When it came time to leave, he piled into our car as if all was understood. We stood outside the elevators in the lobby of my hotel, and when the doors opened, Jake looked at me, I looked back at him, and . . .

Ladies and Gentlemen, we have a winner.

It was done. We both stepped inside as a sign of consent. As if on cue, the rest of our entourage suddenly backed away from the elevator doors, announcing that they were "starving and wanted to grab a bite." They too understood the mating dance that was taking place. And they retreated into the background so that nature could run its course.

Jake and I both knew that they were only taking a lap to give us some privacy. It was 2:00 a.m., and with my friend staying in my room, there were few ways for Steve and Isaac to entertain her before she'd start wanting to head back upstairs for bed. We might've been promiscuous, but we didn't want to be assholes. In order to be courteous, we knew that our time was limited. We hurried to the room and he pretended not to be shocked by the disarray of clothing and suitcases lining the floor.

He climbed on the bed and crawled toward me as I stood at the foot. He helped me take my dress off, but it was a little tight, and when he pulled it over my head and off my arms, the recoil caused me to stumble backward. The heel of my foot caught the edge of the open suitcase, and with no core strength to speak of, I fell immediately back onto the exposed zipper of my Tumi carry-on like a tree felled by Paul Bunyan himself. My romantic night began to vanish before my eyes. I pictured the famous Samsonite ad featuring a circus elephant with one leg on a suitcase and silently prayed the bag beneath me would have the same rebound and resilience. There was no scrambling or flailing of my arms—I was dead weight in a trust fall with no one to catch me. I felt my bare back hit the suitcase, and immediately, without a sound, I pulled myself up with a force I didn't know I had. It was as if God, the great puppeteer, had pulled a marionette's string from my chest and lifted me up. What was once laid flat was now erect and upright, like Lazarus arisen from the dead. It was like the urban legends of a mother finding the strength to lift a car off of a crumpled stroller. Nothing was going to ruin this night for me. I was committed.

Jake looked startled and then aghast. "Are you okay?" he asked, wide-eyed.

I popped one hip, flipped my hair, and readjusted my panties, which had shifted from the sheer force of the fall. "Fine. And you?"

Nothing was going to keep me down. We ripped open the spontaneous romance kit from the minibar—lube, condoms, and something else I can't remember—and did it with the lights on. He got dressed and told me that he'd go downstairs and tell my friend she was free to return upstairs and go to bed. And that I was probably asleep up there already.

"Thanks," I said.

No less than five minutes later, my friend came bounding into the room, wild eyed and curious: "Tell. Me. Everything."

I tousled my unkempt hair over my face and tried to act at least a little coy and coquettish. But before I could even say, "Why, heavens! I don't know what you mean . . ." in my best, most modest impression, she screamed, "THERE'S BLOOD ON THE SHEETS!"

My brain worked at warp speed, running through the last forty-five minutes expediently, trying to figure out where on earth the blood could have come from. I was at a complete loss. We'd had the most basic, vanilla sex of our lives. The kinkiest thing about the hookup was the overhead lighting. Who had been bleeding and why? It felt so undignified.

I remembered my fall from grace flat on my back. Now that the adrenaline of our hookup was wearing off, it was starting to hurt. I turned around and lifted up my shirt.

"Is my back bleeding?" I asked her.

"No," she laughed. "Why would your back be bleeding?"

I explained to her how the force of pulling my tight dress over my head had sent me reeling backward onto the open suitcases. Her hand snapped to her mouth in shock.

"You're kidding me. What did you do?" she asked, appalled.

"I jumped back up!" I explained, "and acted like nothing had happened."

She let out a shocked breath. "Like nothing had happened?" She laughed. "What did HE do?"

"He just went with it, I guess. I didn't give him much of a chance to back out. But maybe I cut up my back when I fell on the suitcase? It really hurts. Are you sure you can't see anything?" I asked again, lifting my shirt even higher.

"No," she said. "I can't see anything. Your back looks fine."

Huh. I was perplexed. What had I done to this man? We left the mystery unsolved, and I gallantly offered to sleep on the side of the bed with the bloodstain. She didn't say it, but I could tell my friend was thinking, *I should've booked that room at the Beverly Hills Hotel.*

The next morning, we woke up late for our flight. The car service was already downstairs waiting to take us to the airport when we realized the time. Still hungover and now groggy from only a few hours of sleep, we began running around the room, throwing things into our open bags.

The room was a disaster and our flight was set to depart in just a few short hours, so we started shoving whatever we could fit into the suitcases splayed open across the floor. I was in the bathroom, stumbling around gathering toiletries, when I heard a scream. Fearing she'd found more blood on the bed, I burst into the room. "What's wrong now?" I asked.

"My ring. I can't find my wedding ring."

I gasped. "Fuck."

Where could it be? Where had we been? What were we going to do? Our flight was leaving, I was barely coherent, and that ring could be anywhere from the photography studio to the limo services to the rooftop bar to Craig's to The Abbey. We didn't have time to go looking or make any calls. I tried to remain calm and help her retrace her steps.

"When was the last time you remember having it on?" I asked.

"I had it on after dinner when we left for The Abbey," she remembered.

Phew. That eliminated a majority of the other locations, so we were in luck. "Where would you have put it? Was it loose on your finger?" My heart was racing. It didn't matter that it wasn't my ring that was lost, I felt absolutely and completely responsible. The ring had been lost under my watch. I had lured her here to help me, I had insisted we go out on the town, I had danced the night away at The Abbey, and I had found the only straight guy there and brought him home for a one-night stand. I was a whore and a harlot and a bad friend, and now I had lost her ring. When you have the morals of an alley cat, these were the consequences. *This is why I can't have nice things.*

I thought of her husband, trusting and kind, and how he would assume she had taken her ring off to appear single so she could cavort freely among the revelers at the club, and how that was my fault too. He'd never let her hang out with me again, and she would always remember this trip with disdain and a pit in her stomach. They'd have to retrace our steps for the insurance claim and my slutty antics would be forever preserved in the annals of some insurance agent's little black notebook. I couldn't bear it. WE HAD TO FIND THE RING!

We dumped out our suitcases and combed through the pockets and nooks and crannies of our bags. Then, we piled it all on top of the blood-stained sheet, and she began crawling on the floor on her hands and knees, combing the thick carpet with her fingers, hoping the ring had fallen down among the fluffy fibers and would pop up when her hands found it. Terror had set in for her as well: she had called her husband (which I begged her not to do) and admitted to him that it was lost. This was no ordinary wedding ring, by the way. It was a four-carat, perfect-clarity, Tiffany-cut princess setting, and its street value if I had to replace it would cost me my entire book advance as well as my dignity.

"Let's say a prayer," I offered. I couldn't believe I was saying the words as I heard them. Prayer had always been my fail-safe go-to when I was in an insurmountable situation. It was my first instinct to call on the divine when I needed a miracle. I knew in my still drunk, barely hanging-on state that I was not going to be able to get myself out of this on my own. I needed backup. And God was the only one available at 7:00 a.m. at the Mondrian in Los Angeles. Our childhood training kicked in, and we both knelt down on the finger-combed carpet, folded our arms, and bowed our heads.

After a beat, my friend opened her eyes, looked at me, and said, "You say it."

"Dear Heavenly Father, we have lost a ring. And we really need to find it. Please help us know where to look so that we can find her ring, make our flight, and return home to our children who need us, Heavenly Father. (Don't make the children suffer because of me!)"

I thought about making deathbed promises in my throes of desperation, but I knew if I didn't buy my promises myself, God would never fall for them either. I closed the prayer with a solid "Amen," and we slowly got up from our knees. I walked back into the bathroom, but I felt helpless. I only prayed when there was nothing left to do, and I wasn't sure God was going to be in a mood to reward me considering what I had been up to the last twenty-four hours: posing for the cover of a book called *Bad Mormon*, drinking at a rooftop bar, drinking at Craig's, drinking AND dancing at The Abbey, and then drinking and dancing in the sheets with a stranger. I was fucked. The ring was as good as gone.

But then, the heavens and the flap of my friend's Chanel bag opened up. And she screamed again: "I FOUND IT!"

"YOU FOUND IT?" I couldn't believe it. I couldn't fucking believe it. My prayer had actually worked! Maybe there was a God! And maybe He was listening and didn't care about my sins. He was still saving me, saving our friendship, saving my reputation, and saving our memories of this trip for the rest of our lives.

"I tucked it into this back flap of my purse, but when I looked before I hadn't seen it. Here it is," she proclaimed. As she placed it on her finger, it sparkled endlessly. We laughed and hugged and then hurriedly finished packing.

By the grace of God and LA traffic, we made it to the airport in the nick of time, only to find that our flight was delayed an hour. I didn't care at all. All had been restored in more than one way. The mystery of the missing ring had been solved with a little divine intervention and faith. But the mystery of the blood on the sheets still remained, and my back was still hurting. With time to spare, we got in line at Jersey Mike's to order a sandwich. There's something special about a six-inch turkey provolone, Mike's Way before 9:00 a.m., and I planned on experiencing it. While we waited in a queue with the other customers, I redirected the attention to my back again. "Are you sure you can't see anything?" I pleaded.

"Here, let me get my glasses out," she offered. I turned around again and gingerly lifted up the back of my shirt.

"OH MY GOSH!" she exclaimed. "NOW I see it! Your back is all cut up with scabs of dried blood. It must've been from the zipper when you fell. That's where the blood came from!"

She laughed, I laughed, and the customers watching us laughed. She had my back that weekend in more ways than one. And God smiled on all of it.

It's funny . . . I had brought my friend out to LA to ensure that the cover shoot for my book was thematically appropriate. But, more importantly, she taught me the true meaning behind its title. In the end, being a Bad Mormon wasn't about spilling sacred secrets, drinking red wine, or jumping on a trampoline with limbs outstretched. Instead, it was about embracing the absurdity of life without judgment and shame.

I carried with me a newfound appreciation for the irreverent spirit that burned and thrived within me and a new understanding of my relationship with the divine. I understood that, at the core of it all, Bad Mormon was just another name for a Good-Time Girl—both of which were no longer labels of shame, but badges of honor.

Now, whenever I tell people the story of my *Bad Mormon* cover shoot, my friends politely interject, "Heather, just say you went to *West Hollywood*. You don't have to say the name of the hotel. I know you loved it, but the Mondrian isn't cool."

EIGHTEEN

EVERYBODY WANTS A KITTEN; NOBODY WANTS A CAT

Even when I want to die on the inside, my cat makes me feel happy on the outside.

I've seen the phrase "happiness is a warm cat" cross-stitched on a pillow somewhere, or laminated on a wood sign in a rerun episode of *My 600-lb Life*. It's a phrase so trite I never considered decorating my home with it, let alone believing it, for God's sake. If someone I respected described happiness to me as a "warm cat," I would consider them to be 100 percent unbearable. Aim higher, dear friend. Your warm-happiness cat, if she's like most cats, probably can't stand you. Not to mention: Isn't that a lot of pressure to put on a house pet, to be your entire source of joy? But I can't help it if it rings true every time I sit down next to . . . well . . . my warm cat and feel what can only be described as pure happiness.

I didn't always have a relationship with my cat. For years, we lived under the same roof before I even knew that she was actually capable of sitting beside me, let alone whether or not she was warm. In the beginning of our relationship, we respected each other's boundaries, which, for the most part, meant that I was her abject servant and she was the abusive master. She reinforced this daily by meowing in the early morning hours if she felt like waking me up just to ignore me. We weren't strangers by any means, but every exchange we shared was hostile on some level. Shared circumstances and shared life goals had thrust us both into each other's orbit and, despite the fact that she clearly couldn't stand me, we were making the best of it. I guess you could say we were, at the very least, "frenemies."

Frenemies can be a tricky relationship to navigate—even more so when one of the parties is an animal—and Grey, my cat, and I were no different. I'd acknowledge and greet her earnestly, and she would occasionally turn her gaze in my direction only to blandly blink or look away as if I weren't speaking to her at all. If I positioned myself nearby and tried to pet her, she would allow me a few strokes before she would stand up, take three or four steps away, and settle back down onto the bed just a fingertip's stretch out of reach. It was both criticism and withholding in its harshest form. When I had guests over, she would immediately hide only to resurface in the eeriest, creepiest ways: slinking from around a corner on the staircase or peering down from a closet ledge with judgmental eyes, letting me and my guests know that she felt both encroached upon and unimpressed.

I tried to force my love on her; I was her owner after all. I bought the wet food and the dry food and alternated them like a seasoned chef; sprinkling in the specialty *Temptations* treats that accosted me with aquarium-like odors every time I opened their sealed foil packages. The smell made me retch, but I made sure to hide it from her, and I never complained. Felt catnip mice and squeaky squirrels don't grow on trees, but as expensive as they may be, I made sure she still had plenty of them to openly ignore and never play with. And I made sure our pantry was stocked with the best mid-priced cat food that Target could offer. I treated her like a queen. I deserved a little compensation, dammit! I wanted to hear her purr and cuddle on my lap. Didn't all my efforts merit a little affection? Didn't she owe me that at least? "Just lay there and let me pet you. I'll be done in a minute. There . . . was that so bad?" She always seemed to enjoy it once it was over.

Whenever I tried to pick her up, she'd twist her body so that her claws threatened my bare skin, ready to pounce away at the first release of my grip. I have a permanent four-inch white scar on my left breast that has never faded. It glares back at me, forever a reminder of a time when our relationship was clouded with violence.

I'd known the love of a pet before, so I knew what I was missing out on. I had experienced the type of instant chemistry and affection that can exist between owner and domesticated animal, but it was hard to hold out hope that my relationship with Grey would ever get there. She was, after all, no Custard.

Custard was my "husband-has-moved-out-and-now-we-can-get-a-new-pet" cat. I adopted Custard during a time of turbulence and upheaval in my personal life, a time where I felt absolutely unfit to parent anything. I knew that my kids wanted a kitten. What three little girls don't? Their dad had moved out, their mom was hanging by a thread, and I was sure that a cute orange tabby would fix it all. Happiness, after all, might just be a warm cat named Custard.

Whenever I came home each night, I'd call his name in a whisper under my breath—"Custard . . . "—and wait in the darkness. I'd hear a thump onto the ground above me as he jumped off the bed, landing on the floor, followed by the soft swish-click of his padded claws as he approached—never rushed or frantic, but regally and without hesitation. Custard was not a proud cat as much as he was noble. He'd curl up on my chest and purr so strongly that I could feel the vibrations in my lungs when I took a deep breath. I'd breathe in and out trying to throw his body off balance, but he would rise and fall with each breath, never flinching or showing any sign of leaving. Thrash as I might, Custard was in it for the long haul. Custard loved me . . . and only me.

He wasn't as loving or generous with the girls. He dismissed their attention and tea parties, and he was critical of their twirling and dancing. I knew they were uncomfortable around him, but I refused to acknowledge it. The children who had desperately wanted a kitten quickly changed their minds when Custard refused to warm to them. They lived in fear and I was blind to it. When Georgia, my six-year-old, began pulling her nightgown down over her bare legs each time she went upstairs, I didn't understand why, until one morning, I witnessed Custard leaping from behind and attacking her calves. "Why is he doing that?" I asked her. "Are you carrying food?" He was so good to me, I couldn't fathom that he was anything less to anyone else.

It was late in the fall, a little over a year into our relationship, when Custard missed his first night at home. He was a rescue cat that had come from a farm, and it never occurred to me to keep him penned up inside. He went where he wanted to go, and we had a sweet routine by the back patio French doors that worked perfectly for us. I'd let him out to roam in our backyard and beyond, and when he finished his wanderings, he'd return and sit patiently by the glass partition waiting for me to let him in. He had never failed to return, so I never questioned his safety. It wasn't until I started to go to bed that I realized he wasn't there. I called out his name, but I didn't hear the familiar sound of his padded feet shuffling anywhere inside the house. I went outside and called for him up and down the street, but there was no response. I didn't give it too much thought. Custard was an adventurous cat, he roamed as he pleased, and this was the first time he had stayed out later than my bedtime. He deserved a little me time, I supposed. And, after all, I trusted him.

The next morning, I expected to hear Custard meowing at the back door, cold and eager to be let inside, but he wasn't there. There was no sign of wet paw prints or fresh scratches on the door frame. Suddenly, I was worried.

When evening rolled around and he still hadn't turned up, I went into full "Bring Him Home" mode. I put some of our clothing on the back patio to remind him of our scent. I put his favorite foods in bowls on the front and back porches to cover wind flow in both directions. I wanted the smells of hearth and home to waft in the breeze and remind him that he had a family that loved him, missed him, and wanted him back no matter the circumstances. But nothing. The food went untouched, and the clothes grew stiff in the increasingly cold night air.

By night three, I was sleeping out on the couch in close proximity to the back patio so that if he cried out I would hear. I was heartbroken.

On the fourth morning, I got a phone call that shattered my world: Custard had been found. Animal Services had received a report of an orange tabby cat hit on the side of the road less than a half-block from our house. The crew had found Custard and brought him into the shelter. There had been a frost the night before and they wanted his body to be discovered before the next snowfall. They had identified him by the microchip we had embedded in his ear as a kitten, and they called us as soon as they could.

I cried more over Custard's death than I had over my husband's leaving. It felt like true heartbreak—a unilateral, uncomplicated grief. I wept when I had to tell my daughters. It was the first time we'd ever discussed death, and all of the soothing things I had learned about the afterlife in Mormonism didn't seem to apply. There was no relief, no Rainbow Bridge to carry me from loss to acceptance. Custard had healed a broken part of me, and now he was gone.

I cried openly and uncontrollably, and since I was crying about the cat and not their father or their future, I cried in front of my kids, and they cried with me. I had put on a happy face as much as possible in the months after their dad left, careful to keep a stiff upper lip and not upset the balance of their lives any further, but the loss of Custard released the floodgates. I could cry like the wailing women in the Bible with sackcloth and ashes and feel unashamed. My grief surprised even me; it was just a cat, after all. Pull yourself together.

And then there was Grey.

Grey came to live with us as a rebound and replacement cat, and my heart was never quite in it. When enough time had passed after Custard's death, my kids began feeling brave enough to suggest a new kitten. I agreed to take them to the Humane Society to "just look," and I made no promises. In my mind, Custard was a once-in-a-lifetime cat; any other feline would pale in comparison. But once we got to the animal shelter, the girls zeroed in on Grey almost immediately. The volunteers had labeled her as a "rescue" and her breed as Russian Blue. I saw Russian Blue on her paperwork and thought it sounded elite, expensive. Now I was interested. I immediately googled "Russian Blue rescue" to see if it was even a possibility. A purebred collector's cat roaming the streets? It was just romantic enough to consider. Maybe she was a diamond in the rough? A designer bag mismarked at HomeGoods.

I agreed to bring her home, but I was just going through the motions to appease my kids. A few weeks after we got her acclimated, her bright blue eyes, a trademark of the breed, began to transition to a glowing green: an indication that she was not a purebred but a tabby mix and therefore would never win any awards at the CFA International Cat Show. Her street value plummeted. She must've felt my disappointment because, as she shifted from kitten to cat, she failed to bond with me or any of the kids. She kept to herself and treated us like shit. She never let us hold or pet her, and she only acknowledged us when she needed her bowls filled with food and water. And even then she still drank out of the toilet bowl.

I thought Grey would always be an asshole. I worked on our relationship with toys and treats, I pleaded and promised, I whispered and cajoled, but she always just retreated and ignored me. The same love I'd had with Custard was proving unfathomable for Grey, her demeanor as dark and stormy as her shiny coat. The girls and I even discussed getting rid of her in hushed conversations when things got really bad. She had a peeing-in-the-sink phase that I never thought I would survive. The veterinarian said it might just be that she liked the feeling of the cold bowl against her privates, but I doubted that theory. Grey didn't like anything except seeing me recoil when I walked to the bathroom sink and smelled cat pee.

I started googling dark things like "Life expectancy of Russian Blue cats," "Cats from shelters: how long will they live?" and "Re-homing for angry cats." I finally resigned myself that we would be living together but separate and accepted that there was no real connection. We were coexisting as less than amicable roommates. But if "happiness is a warm cat" didn't land before, I could now put up a sign that said "Unhappiness is a cold-ass cat," and the tension in our home was thick.

Just as I was thinking I had been saddled with the worst cat in the world, the universe came knocking on my door to show me that it could always be worse.

It was a beautiful fall afternoon, and I was working in my kitchen. Grey was nowhere to be seen, per usual. I had opened the back door in order to let the crisp fall air flow through the house. I was well into my meeting when a pained meow emerged from somewhere inside. It wasn't a meow that I recognized, and my body stiffened in fear. "Grey?" I called out timidly. In reply, I heard an even louder, more strained yowl that could only have come from Grey if she was in pain or in labor.

I timidly walked out of the kitchen and around the corner toward the sound. As soon as I turned into the hallway, I realized who and what was making that awful noise: there, crouched on the top ledge of our basement staircase, was a horrifying creature. This did not appear to be a cat or any other animal that I immediately recognized—it was flesh-toned and wrinkly and had wiry hairs sprouting from its little shriveled apple face. Its bony tail thrashed, and it cowered and crouched into the staircase, hissing directly at me. I let out a bloodcurdling scream, and the creature responded by leaping the four descending stairs in one bound. It was trembling now, frightened by its strange surroundings and my screams and retreated further into the house and down the staircase into our basement.

"HELP! HELP! HELP!" I screamed, to no one in particular. I was home alone, and except for my colleague who was listening to everything via my abandoned Zoom meeting, there was no one around to help me. I could recognize now that it was a cat, and a cat someone cared about because it had a collar. But I wasn't sure if I should be afraid of the creature itself or any human that would want to actually own it. Were they somewhere inside my house too? I needed to get rid of it, but I didn't know how. I wasn't about to pick it up. It was a specific hairless breed, a Sphynx cat, which I had only seen in movies— *Austin Powers* to be exact, and it was the type of cat that only Dr. Evil could love or even touch, for that matter.

I ran back to the kitchen and saw, in my peripheral vision, the open patio door and realized too late that the cat had crept in unnoticed right behind my back. My colleague on the Zoom call had heard my screams and frantically asked if they should call 911. "YES! NO! I DON'T KNOW!" I screamed. I was in a full blown panic. I needed to corral it and chase it out through the same door it had entered. But now, it was cornered in the basement, and we were well past the stage of me luring it with sweet cat calls or a bowl of food. And speaking of cat food, where was Grey? Did she know this cat had crossed over into her terrain? Would she be willing to chase her out for me?

I grabbed a broom from the pantry. In my mind, I would scream and threaten and use the broom to herd the creature back up the stairs, around the corner, and out into the crisp fall air from whence it came. I'd seen this method performed in cartoons in my youth, and I was pretty sure it was a method I could manage. But, as I approached, broom in hand, the cat meowed and scampered farther down the stairs and straight into my youngest daughter's bedroom. I slammed the door shut, trapping it inside her room, and breathed a sigh of relief. At least now it was contained, and I had time to come up with a plan. There was nothing in her room that it could hurt or damage.

Then . . . I remembered: the guinea pig.

Weren't Sphynx cats predators of small rodents? I remembered the cats in an old Disney cartoon and thought about the eerie way they moved and had tried to climb into the baby's crib. If furry cats were a danger to babies, then surely hairless cats were a danger to defenseless guinea pigs. I had to get it out of there . . . and fast.

Within minutes of the intrusion, the girls arrived home from school and found me hyperventilating on the staircase holding a broom. They looked frightened. And I, in my frenzy, forgot one of the rules of parenting: never let them see you panic.

"HELP!" I screamed as they walked through the door and dumped their backpacks. "We have an intruder! There's a hairless cat trapped in your bedroom and it's about to eat your guinea pig." I didn't spare their feelings as I explained the situation. The girls stared back at me in shock, trying to process how they were expected to help.

"Should I just go into my room and see if I can coax it out?" Annabelle, thirteen, asked matter-of-factly. She clearly did not understand what she was facing.

"It calls itself a cat, but there is nothing warm or happy about it. It's an angry hairless creature with guinea pig murder on its brain," I warned. But she ignored me and went down into her room. Using the flashlight on her phone, she found the animal crouched under her bed. With some well-practiced patience, she got it to come out just far enough for her to gingerly pick it up and carry it upstairs. I couldn't even look. She placed it on the back patio, and it scampered away, the bells on its collar jingling. The guinea pig was unaffected, but I was still shaken.

This experience with the Sphynx precipitated a mighty change in my relationship with Grey. After the hairless cat left, all I wanted to do was be rejected by *my* cat: a recognizable ball of fur. Our relationship was complicated, but at least I still wanted to touch her.

I don't know who changed first, if it was my appreciation of her or the other way around, but something in the air shifted after that day. She started coming around more often, sitting on my bed, following me into a room, sleeping by my side for a few hours a day, especially after the house cleaners had come and made the bed. She'd ignore my room for the rest of the week when it was unkempt and tousled with sheets, clothes, and blankets, but she loved a freshly made bed and enjoyed it whenever she had the chance.

With time, Grey's initial disdain faded into acceptance, and that acceptance faded into appreciation, and appreciation has since evolved into something much more. When she is sitting beside me now, we have what feels deeper than just happiness. It might even be love.

Now when I climb into bed, she sometimes will follow me. I'll see the door creep open, and my heart will skip a beat. If I come on too strong or call out to her too quickly, she will turn around and saunter out of my room. But if I time it right and show just the right balance of welcomeness and boundaries, she will leap onto my bed and even curl up by my side. If I touch or talk to her too much, she will walk to the edge and curl up with her back toward me. It's a silent but effective rejection. She's not a fan of demonstrative love, and when I go too far, she lets me know. She can't fool me, though: I know her love for me has grown in kind to mine. When the summer months roll around, she's the first to bring me her kills and vomits, and I respond like a proud parent to both. I wouldn't want her to think our love is anything but unconditional.

We all want that young, affectionate, exciting love—the warm happiness you can only get from a kitten. It's fun while it lasts, but it's not sustainable. Everybody wants a kitten; nobody wants a cat.

I may have thought I just wanted to survive on the effortless love I had with Custard—something easy, attainable, and willingly given—but what I really want is the type of relationship I have with Grey. A love that is a slow burn, that is well-earned, that I never thought I'd like, but that I'd now be devastated to lose.

NINETEEN

A BULL SHARK IN POUGHKEEPSIE

Growing up, my dad took us on plenty of road trips and plenty of rivers. We would take white-water rafting trips on the Colorado and the Green, and as we got older, we ventured into the San Juan and Snake rivers where the rapids proved more challenging. My dad was a talented river guide and outdoorsman, and he knew how to be a great host in the great outdoors—a fellow showman, if you will. One of the most important things he taught us once we began navigating boats on the water ourselves, was how to "read a river."

Before every major rapid, we'd pull out a little upstream, tie our boats off on shore, and get out to assess the waters we were about to paddle through. If you went down the rapid without evaluating it first, you wouldn't be aware of the hidden obstacles—the sleeper rocks hiding under the froth of a wave, or the sinkholes that lurked underneath the biggest rapids. All perils that once you discovered them might be too late to avoid. Studying the currents and evaluating the ride from afar is what my dad called "reading a river," and in order to do it correctly, you had to leave your boat, get out of the swirling waters, and stand firmly on the shore.

Now that I've had some distance from things in my own personal life, I realize that this metaphor is greater than a safe-rafting protocol. In fact, when I think about my life, I find it easy to compare it to a journey downriver. But in my case—the case of somebody who grew up in a high-demand faith community that preached binary, black-and-white, good-and-evil thinking—I can't help but think that I'm perhaps less like a river, and more like an estuary—like the Hudson.

The Hudson River is, like the name suggests, a river. But with its brackish water and changing tides leading into the Atlantic, it has been called not just a river, but a "river that flows both ways." Which, of course, makes things a little more complicated.

The first time I visited New York City, I was aware that the Hudson River was a "thing," but I never actually understood where or what it was . . . And I definitely didn't know it was an estuary. When I looked at the water from the West Side Highway, I assumed I was just looking at the Atlantic Ocean. I don't think I even realized that it was the Hudson River until Captain Sully landed his plane on it.

The Hudson was unlike any river I had ever seen. I only knew rivers to be freshwater streams with sandy banks that climbed steeply into the mountains, like the ones I had rafted down with my dad. Rivers where you could fish for trout and search for tadpoles. I had never known a river to have tides, or marine life, or giant barges and steamer ships like I saw on the Hudson. I had certainly never seen a river wide enough to land a 747, let alone a river that flowed both ways. But that's exactly what the Hudson River was.

The Hudson River flows not just from the bustling metropolis of Manhattan but all the way up to the Adirondack Mountains, far away from anything a New Yorker or wayward sea life would ever recognize. But one time, it was reported that a bull shark was discovered swimming upstate in the pure waters outside of Poughkeepsie. Everyone marveled at the shark's ability to survive in between the toxicity of the salty sea and the fresh water that called to him.

The experience of being caught "in-between" was not new to me, and I identified with that shark. I've always been a little good and a little bad, a little salty and a little fresh. And because of these intersecting and, at times, conflicting parts of myself, I've struggled to navigate the changing tides and ever-shifting direction of swimming in a river that flows both ways. I've failed to "read the river" on more than one occasion, too caught up in the current to put any significant distance between myself and my circumstances. Instead of looking for hidden sleeper rocks and sinkholes, I neglected to notice red flags and warning signs about relationships that wound up taking a significant toll on my life.

Now that I'm on the other side standing safely on shore, I can look back and reflect on how I sometimes failed to read the river. In other words, I have only been able to process the trauma of leaving the church once I was out of it. And the same can be said about many of my relationships, including my friendship with my former *Housewives* castmate Jen Shah.

I was what they call a cradle Mormon—someone born into the faith. It was all I ever knew. It was quite literally the air I breathed at home and church and, to some extent, in school and my wider community. There were many pivotal times in my life when I was shown another path, a different way to live, and yet I always inevitably chose to remain in the church rather than leave.

When my husband left our marriage, I was given an opportunity to start fresh. I was drinking and dating and living a double life, but I chose to keep up all the appearances of being a Good Mormon. I had friends who had left the church and were starting over wild and free, but I counseled them against it, and I continued to cling to the patterns that I thought would keep me safe and keep me happy. When there was a fork in the road, I chose the well-trodden path Every. Single. Time.

I used to believe that it was God's will and my ardent testimony that pulled me back into the fold—the truth of the Gospel that I could not outrun or detach myself from. But with time and distance, I'm learning that it has very little to do with faith, and it has everything to do with behavior and belonging.

I've read that cults prey on the vulnerable, but even though I never saw myself as a vulnerable person or a victim, my experience in the church is no different. As missionaries, we sought out the downtrodden, the poor, the meek souls willing to listen to our sweet message of hope. We told ourselves that it was only the poor in spirit who could hear the still, small voice of the Holy Ghost. But too often, the poor in spirit also tended to be the poor in money. It's not that we promised joining the church would make anyone rich—because it wouldn't. (In fact, joining the church will cost you 10 percent of your income in tithes.) Instead, we promised that the vulnerabilities in a person's life—especially financial vulnerabilities—and the voids that they created would be filled in "different" ways.

When you join the church, you are immediately included in a highly organized, highly attentive family of very kind, very good-hearted people. You are assigned a "visiting" and a "home" teacher who both check on you once a month, and you are introduced to a local bishop who offers guidance and support. Your children are immediately integrated into a youth group, with Sunday-school lessons taught weekly by leaders who are engaged and excited and dedicated to making the Church of Jesus Christ of Latter-Day Saints look like fun! "MAKE CHURCH GREAT AGAIN" is practically emblazoned on their red baseball caps. You could say that on the day you get baptized, you become rich in EVERYTHING except money and time. When you have financial independence, it's much easier to feel less vulnerable in all of the other ways—socially, structurally—and you're less likely to fall victim to the institution.

The same is true for reality television. When casting began for *The Real Housewives of Salt Lake City*, the OG cast consisted of me, Whitney Rose, Meredith Marks, Lisa Barlow, and Mary Cosby. Casting was incomplete because we were missing the spark that a good sizzle reel is dependent on. They were looking for a very specific someone. So when casting directors began asking us for more names, I offered up Jen Shah's. She was a frequent customer at my business, Beauty Lab + Laser, and would come in for all of our latest treatments overdressed in furs and Gucci tracksuits. I didn't know her very well, but she had the look of someone I'd want to watch on TV. I had an employee reach out and ask her if she was interested in filming for an untitled reality show based in SLC. She readily agreed.

Once Jen signed on to film, we were off like gangbusters. She was the missing piece that they needed and, at the time, it was easy to believe that there was no show without her.

When I was cast on *The Real Housewives*, it was during a very vulnerable time: I was a recently divorced, struggling entrepreneur and a single mom raising three preteen daughters. My entire life had imploded, and I had no sense of direction and no hope for a palatable future. Add to that that I was at my highest weight since high school, and you have the Housewife hot mess that they were looking for. I had barely been able to assess the wreckage of my divorce and my leaving the church as cameras were up and rolling. By the time I realized I needed to "read the river," it was already too late. I couldn't get out of the swirling waters to see anything except the next wave about to crash over my head.

It was like I left one cult and was recruited right away into another. I was stuck in the river that flows both ways—with each stroke of progress, the tide turned and brought me right back down to where I'd started.

I was being given the opportunity of a lifetime, but it came with strings attached, just like everything. It was a chance to live the big, extraordinary life I had dreamed of since I was a little girl—a Plan of Happiness that had never been presented to me before, an alternate path that was too tempting to turn away from. It was a Golden Ticket, but it came at a price.

The one thing that kept me from wanting to go on *The Real Housewives* was what I would have to give up. I knew that I could no longer pretend to be a member of the church and that my faith crisis would be exposed. I knew that if I went on a show like this, I would lose my family, my community, and possibly my salvation. But I went willingly into the fight, almost consciously, knowing it was a predicament fraught with peril. This was a chance to extend my existence beyond the walls of my own home. A chance to be a part of something bigger and flashier and more exciting than a church Relief Society. This was a chance to experience things that I'd never get to experience otherwise. To be a part of something creative and collaborative and enduring. A legacy of something beyond myself and the bubble I lived in.

It was no different with my friendship with Jen. I knew that if I was friends with her and if I did this show with her, I could be losing my dignity, but at the time it seemed worth the risk. Even if I saw her for who she was, I didn't care because she represented so much of what I wanted.

We had only been hanging out a few weeks when Jen flew off the handle for the first time. We were on a group chat with a mutual friend, and I was talking to Jen about filming for the upcoming sizzle reel. She had been excited and enthused about the process from the beginning, but in this instant, she raged in ALL CAPS: *"IF YOU ARE FUCKING SETTING ME UP I WILL DESTROY YOUR BUSINESS, YOUR FAM-ILY, YOUR WHOLE GODDAMN LIFE. I will not rest until everything you love is destroyed."*

"Fuck this," I replied and left the group chat. I quickly screen-shot the tirade and sent it over to our production team. *"How am I supposed to handle this?"* I asked. This was not what I'd signed up for. I assumed Jen would get in trouble or be reprimanded or quit the show or maybe even be fired, but none of that came to pass. I waited for someone, any-one, to say something about it, but no one did, including Jen.

Casually, the next day she texted me directly as if the tantrum had never occurred: *"Are we still making a show or what?"* she asked. I knew what I was getting into, but I didn't retreat.

"Sure," I replied.

Her tirade was never mentioned again.

Jen was the complete opposite of the type of leaders I was used to following. She represented everything that I was told was wrong about the world, and yet she seemed to be thriving. I was drawn to the phenomenon. She was anathema to everything I had been taught to be, and I had no way to navigate our relationship. I was up a river without a paddle, and the current was too hard to read from within.

I inherited Jen as a castmate, and our show's success felt very codependent on her presence. I had many opportunities along the way to dump Jen, to disavow her terrible deeds, and to distance myself from the stink that seemed to follow her, but I always chose to remain blindly loyal, defending her, protecting her, and refusing to leave.

When she got arrested and the evidence began mounting against her, I did exactly what I had done when confronted with negative things about the church: I turned a blind eye and a blind conscience to the facts. I leaned into loyalty and I leaned into denial (it's not just a river in Egypt). I refused to look into the corners of my mind or the file boxes full of evidence indicating her guilt. Jen would weep and plead and promise that she was absolutely innocent of the charges. She claimed that the trial was a witch hunt because of her success on the show. She cried about being a polarizing figure, a woman of color being unfairly targeted and singled out. She swore on her family, her children's lives, her father's grave, "I AM INNOCENT!!!" And regardless of whether or not she was, she wasn't going anywhere. No one seemed to be firing her anytime soon, and the worse she acted, the more her popularity grew. She was very much a part of our cast, a part of our show, and a part of our lives. She was arrested on a Tuesday and was filming again the following Monday. If the network and the crew didn't seem affected by the charges, who was I as their employee to draw a line in the sand? I couldn't cut her off even if I had wanted to because we were filming a

TV show together, so I'd rather be on her good side than on her very volatile, explosive bad side. It wasn't smart or stupid; it was just the only thing I knew how to do. It was fucking survival.

As Jen received more and more attention regarding her impending criminal trial, her emotional mood swings grew more and more intense. She would blow up at the drop of a hat, and we were defenseless in the face of her tantrums. The dysfunction of our relationship was exposed when I woke up during our season 3 cast trip to San Diego with a black eye. The night before, the women and I had been partying and drinking after the cameras went down. When I woke up the following morning, I didn't remember any of the previous night's antics, but I knew something must've happened because, "Holy shit, look at my eye."

When Jen came into my room that morning, the first thing she said to me was, "Did I do that to you?" I didn't know. I had no idea how I had gotten it, but it wouldn't have mattered even if I did. I didn't really blame anyone but myself.

Later that afternoon, she came back into my room and confessed that she felt responsible. "I got you. Don't worry," I replied without thinking. I was so hungover and so humiliated; I just wanted the whole thing to go away. I refused to see a doctor and I refused to talk about it with any of the producers. The network was concerned and did a full and thorough investigation. When I was interrogated, I plead the fifth. I didn't remember, and I didn't want to talk about it. I refused to reveal any of my conversations with Jen. I felt like I was protecting her, but moreover I felt like I was protecting myself.

A black eye was nothing compared to the emotional torment I felt trying to navigate that friendship. Lisa Barlow said it best: Jen Shah gave all of us a black eye every single day. She wounded us with her lies, with her crimes, with her erratic behavior both on and off screen. But we felt stuck with her, and we loved her. As strange as that sounds, Jen sucked all of us in, especially me. Her capacity to be crazy was equally matched with her capacity to show compassion and her capacity to be kind. And she was funny. She could make us laugh as much as she could make us cry. We were committed. Committed to the show and committed to each other. And despite everything, Jen was a big part of that.

I was ashamed that I had gotten blackout drunk. I was ashamed that I had a black eye. And I was scared at what might happen if there was evidence that Jen had caused it intentionally. I didn't want to admit to myself or anyone else that it might've been intentional, because it was too humiliating. And the truth is, Jen was so out of control that nothing she did ever really felt intentional, just random acts of fucking violence at every turn.

But more than anything, I was embarrassed. I was embarrassed that I had drunk so much that I couldn't remember getting hurt; I was embarrassed that I had ridden so hard for a woman who didn't deserve it; and I was embarrassed that I had been vulnerable enough to let something like this happen in the first place, much less in front of the cameras. My default emotional response was denial. I tried to make a few dumb jokes and deflect the seriousness of the situation, but the more you try to hide and protect yourself from the truth, the bigger the cover-up becomes.

When I was deep in the trenches of Mormonism, denial was my natural reaction to learning of the church's problematic doctrine and tradition. I turned a blind eye and a deaf ear to any and all negativity and operated from a position of ignorant bliss. To not question was the only way I could survive, and I was good at it. No amount of proof or testimony could have swayed me into leaving because the darkness and loneliness that existed on the other side was too frightening to face. When I woke up with a black eye, that pattern repeated. My immediate defense was to deny, deny, deny. I never considered revealing Jen's supposed confession, because the fear of confronting her, exposing her, and losing her friendship was equally as terrifying.

I had given up everything to pursue this second lease on life. I knew the emptiness that existed post-Mormonism, and I wasn't willing to risk experiencing that same hollow feeling post-*Housewives*. So, I doubled down. I was trapped in the competing tides of a brackish estuary. When the river got rough because I failed to read it, I mistakenly believed that the most noble thing to do was go down with the ship.

When discussing her federal charges, the first time Jen ever changed her "I'M INNOCENT, GODDAMMIT" script was the morning she pleaded guilty. I had just been filming with her in New York the day before. Meredith and I had flown out to meet her and to discuss the details of her case and trial that were set to begin the following Monday. Bravo put us up in a beautiful hotel right behind St. Patrick's Cathedral in Midtown Manhattan. Jen stayed in the penthouse suite, with a full wall of panoramic windows looking west to the mighty Hudson River. Before we shot our final scene that weekend, I sat with Jen in her room as the sun set over both the river and her time as an innocent woman. As she sat there in a chair looking out on the city and river below, makeup artists and hairstylists buzzed around her. She wore the hotel's robe, and she seemed serene, calm, and powerful. Unmoving. There was no fear, no tremor, no sign that she was about to admit to fraud and face time in prison. Either she hadn't known how she would plea at that time, or she was living deep within the schisms of her own denial. She sat as stoic as the Mormon church, so sure in their archaic doctrine despite its known harm. She seemed immovable, bigger than the crimes she was accused of, more famous than the federal government itself. And it was easy to hide behind the fortress.

Yet in that moment, as I watched Jen put on all her glam, I saw the woman beneath it all. She looked small in front of the windows, her hands placed gently on her knees as she watched the sun set the room ablaze. While her presence was undoubtedly domineering, there was something almost soft about the humanity that seeped through the veneer of perfection. She too, I realize now, was maybe just as "in-between" as me.

I flew home the next day and had just arrived back in Utah the morning that everything changed. My phone rang around 5:00 a.m. MST. It was Jen and she was sobbing. She could barely get the words out, and her phrasing was so broken that I found myself taking deep breaths as if I could somehow fill her lungs remotely.

"It's okay," I reassured her. "Just breathe. What's going on?"

"Heather," she sobbed, "I have to plead guilty. I have to do it for my family. I can't do this to Sharrieff. I have no choice. I just wanted you to know. Please call Meredith and tell her."

Even in that final moment of vulnerability, she still couldn't admit her guilt or her accountability in any of it. When I read the news report of what she admitted to in open court, my jaw fell open.

I wasn't shocked that she had been capable of committing the crimes she copped to. I had seen her capacity for awfulness, experienced it firsthand, and I knew she lacked character in every way. It was easy to see how she could slip from cretin to criminal. What shocked me was that she was admitting to it. I can only dream the church will one day do the same. She was publicly stating in front of a judge and packed courtroom that she had known that what she was doing was wrong yet she continued to do it. She sought out elderly victims, she played on their naiveté, she signed them up for websites when they didn't own a computer, and she sold them on expensive monthly subscription services that they would never use. And then she billed them relentlessly until they were bankrupt or dead.

I had come up with a thousand different ways for her to be innocent. But I had never considered the thousand different ways that she was guilty. She always got away with everything. Why would I assume these charges to be any different? Maybe she wasn't aware of the sales tactics her call center was using. Maybe most of the people she sold products to bought into the programs knowingly, but she was being prosecuted for the rogue crimes of a few bad actors. I was used to doing mental gymnastics like this in order to make the preposterous seem logical as a member of the church: maybe Brigham Young really did need fifty-six wives. Maybe a top hat and magic stones really were a special way for Joseph Smith to talk to God. Maybe polygamy really was better for the women—after all, who wants to do the dishes alone? When it came to making sense of Jen's crimes, I did the very same thing.

I didn't think she was a mastermind. I didn't think she was rich enough to have the millions they claimed she had stolen. I had never seen her fly to Kosovo or the Cayman Islands, where they claimed she had operations. I had only seen her dancing and drunk and surrounded by assistants. And then there was her commitment to proclaiming her innocence. And not just to me, but to the whole goddamn world, and on television! If Jen hadn't cracked under Andy Cohen's questions at the reunions for Seasons 1 and 2, why would she crack now in front of a grand jury? She had asked all of us for money and had actually borrowed money from people I assumed she'd be embarrassed not to pay back. And none of it fazed her. I could not fathom a situation where she would walk into a courtroom and say, "Well, you were right. I did it. I did it all and I'm willing to admit to it."

The only scenario I could imagine was her fighting for weeks in a packed courtroom and repeating the patterns we had seen over and over again for the last year: "I'm FUCKING INNOCENT. You have to believe me." What I could not see was her admitting that everything she had said and done to prove herself innocent had been an act, and we had all fallen for it. I had read her wrong. I saw the dangers in the stream, but I thought I was finding ways to avoid confronting them. A sleeper rock is harmless to a raft if the water level is high enough or if you hit it just right. It's most dangerous when you creep up on it unaware and the jagged edge tears through the floor of your boat, ripping your world apart and putting your life in peril.

The only thing that woke me up was realizing that I didn't need them to survive. I can finally understand the control that the church and Jen had over me. With time and distance, I'm able to get out of the swirling waters, stand on the bank, and "read the river" for what it was: toxic as fuck.

Leaving is never easy. Just like I don't want to throw away my faith because it feels dismissive of the person I was, it feels equally as hard to throw away my relationship with Jen because of the history we share. But just as I'm done making excuses for the Mormon church, I'm done making excuses for her. I only wish I'd had the strength and awareness to see things for what they were much sooner.

It's not a new thing to be uncomfortable in the "in-between." God Himself said in Revelations, *"I know thy works, that thou art neither cold nor hot. So then because thou art lukewarm, I will spue thee out of my mouth."* I once believed that my own in-betweenness made me lukewarm and toxic. Neither hot nor cold, I was someone that God would spit out if he had to. My ambition and my passions were constantly holding me back, undermining my righteousness. It felt like every time I let the two selves get close, they would bump into each other like the brackish water of a river's estuary. Every time I tried to swim upstream toward the fresh-water source, the tide would change and I'd be pulled back out to sea. I survived in both environments, but I always felt out of place, never quite at home in one or the other. I was a bull shark in Poughkeepsie.

I'm still working every day to sift through the teachings and defense mechanisms that I internalized as a member of the LDS church for over four decades. After all, patterns repeat, and it takes a ton of work to unlearn implicit behaviors. I understand now that true freedom and power begin with refusal. Refusal to betray myself in order to please other people. I'm getting more comfortable with saying, "No. Never again." The more lessons I learn from leaving, the stronger I feel to swim upstream.

TWENTY

MRS. ANGIE KATSANEVAS

Let me tell you a little bit about my friend Angie Katsanevas. She is a consummate hostess, a caretaker, a social butterfly, a talker, a pleaser, and the worst wingman you will ever meet.

I suppose a lot of her misfiring can be attributed to the fact that she hasn't been single in over thirty years. She's lived practically her entire adult life as a married woman. She met her husband, Shawn, at hair school. They joined forces and scissors and never looked back. This means she was never on the singles scene. Perhaps it is precisely for this reason that she feels compelled to *make* a scene every time she's with me, a single woman, in any public place where there may be, by horrible luck or circumstance, a single man somewhere in the vicinity. That's pretty much the only criterion Angie uses for her prospective matchmaking.

"Hey there, handsome," she'll say to the ninety-year-old being wheeled by a caregiver into the Olive Garden. "I don't see a ring on your wrinkled finger. Are you single? Let me introduce you to my friend . . ."

If he can't hear, she'll prompt his caregiver to whisper-shout every-thing into his ear—"She asked if you're single, Jerry."

"What's that?" he replies in confusion.

"SHE WANTS TO KNOW IF YOU'RE SINGLE."

Angie will take any pause as an affirmation and spring into action, gesturing for the caretaker to wheel him on over while I'm forced to stand there frozen with an open-mouthed grimace, willing the very earth I'm standing on to swallow me whole and make me disappear.

"Hi, Jerry," Angie will say, leaning in. "This is my friend Heather. She's single too!"

Angie is so overjoyed by the prospect of a connection that it takes her a few minutes to observe and realize that perhaps she has spoken too soon. Usually, it's a little detail that she overlooked in haste that gives her pause. It can be something as simple as someone needing to remove his dentures in order to eat lunch, or asking if I charge by the hour, or an introduction to his wife. No matter the cause, once she realizes that she may have selected the wrong suitor, panic sets in. Despite the fact that she's as sharp as a tack, her mouth moves much faster than her brain, and the recognition of my deep incompatibility with her chosen suitor comes far too late, usually after we're halfway done penciling in a dinner date.

It's like Angie's living in a life-sized matchmaking game. She walks into a room and assesses everyone immediately like a writer diagram-ming a sentence. Each person is a word that needs to be part of an exclamation, a phrase, or a complete sentence. She has no tolerance for the dangling participle. If there is a woman in the room unpaired, she can sense it like a chef missing a dash of salt. Her palate is prepared for the paired only, and she cannot tolerate the imbalance of a side dish when the entire meal is already plated. A single person at our age is an afterthought jar of pickles casually placed on an already plated, elegant four-course meal.

She has tried repeatedly to set me up with an old high school friend of ours who recently got divorced. She mentioned this prospect so much that I began to hope for a potentially positive outcome, until I by chance ran into him one day and he introduced me to his pregnant girlfriend. "Oh, that's right," Angie admitted, disappointed when I told her the news. She seemed to be considering this predicament for the first time, as if having a nascent ex-wife and a girlfriend with-child were as banal as us discovering that he was a Capricorn. "Is that a deal breaker?"

And then there was the ex-con who was recovering from bladder cancer. "But don't worry," she explained. "The surgery is done laparo-scopically and they don't even go near the penis." These were unfortu-nately not the type of comforting words I wanted to hear while getting set up on a date. I didn't know if I'd be interested in a man whose blad-der wasn't near his penis. I mean, I know beggars can't be choosers, but she didn't even try to spin the pitch in a way that allowed me to retain my dignity.

At BravoCon in Las Vegas, we decided to meet up for a little after-hours gambling. I only had winning at craps on my mind, but Angie was hoping to help me score in another arena. Every activity involving the opposite sex is an opportunity for Angie to bring out her full Yenta. At the casino in Mandalay Bay, it was a feeding frenzy. She scoured the craps table when we first arrived, and I saw the moment when she real-ized that we were surrounded by men. When it was my turn to roll and the stickman passed me the dice, I saw her eyes light up.

"Woohoo! I sense a connection here. Did you see how he slid those dice right over to you? We-ell-ell, someone is feeling frisky. Come on, Heather, roll an eight and I'll get him for you . . ." Angie cooed. "I'm sorry, what's your name, sir?"

The graying fifty-year-old career dealer, without looking up from the table, pointed to his company-issued name tag reading "Thomas," and continued racking the chips.

"Thomas! Do you see that, Heather? His name is Thomas. What a great name! Do you like that name, Heather? Heather and Thomas sound great together, don't they? It's got a nice ring to it. It would look great on a wedding invitation. I can see your Christmas cards now: *Season Greetings from Heather and Thomas.*"

All of this is happening right in front of me, to me, and all around me. There is no safe place to hide. No ejection button. No aborting the mission. I can't deny Thomas, this poor man who has done nothing wrong except show up for his shift as scheduled and is now trying to keep track of the bets dropped by the fifteen drunken finance bros hurling casino chips and insults as fast as their swollen tongues and bulging wallets can muster.

But I really can't blame her. If I was going to roll the dice on finding a catch among all the fish in the sea, Mandalay Bay in Las Vegas wasn't a bad place to start. If I was gonna get lucky anywhere, wouldn't it be here? Maybe she saw something in Thomas the Stickman that I had yet to discover. And, if his forearm tattoo told me anything, it was that he was much more than just a craps dealer; he also was a man who loved his mom and apparently eagles.

It also didn't hurt that the dice were hot for our game. We were winning every hand, pass line, hard four, and hard eight; we couldn't lose. I made sure to generously tip Thomas not only for the humiliation of being subjected to Angie's incessant matchmaking, but also to let him know that the more I kept winning and the more drinks they kept serving, the more her suggestion seemed increasingly attractive.

When it was Angie's turn to throw the dice, she used it as her personal opportunity to take the figurative microphone and involve the rest of the table in her quest to get me coupled: "Don't you guys think they'd make a great couple? Wouldn't they be so cute together? Thomas, are you single? I don't see a ring on that finger."

Thomas, like any experienced dealer with a drunken guest, said, "Oh, there's a ring in my heart."

Angie didn't miss a beat: "A ring in your heart? What's her name?"

Thomas looked right at me and said, "Heather."

JACKPOT!

Just like a good game of craps, love has the power to make you feel alive. The rush of the unknown, the possibility of hitting it big, and the potential to walk away with a fortune are all attributes of both gambling and romance. Angie—and apparently Thomas—recognized these parallels all too well, and they were ready to risk it all just so long as I could pony up enough courage to really buy into this whole lovers experiment.

Thomas wasn't bad looking. In fact, he looked a bit like Kenny Rogers, pre-facelift and post-Roasters. Staring at him with his long, hooked wooden stick from across the table made me hungry for more than just a fried chicken and butter biscuit combo. Maybe Angie was right, our names *would* look good together on a wedding invitation . . . And with an ordained Elvis impersonator just a few doors down, what did I really have to lose that hadn't already been lost before?

But just as I was writing the vows in my head, a hunched older man with a jet-black toupee and oversized vest came over to the table and tapped Thomas—*my* Thomas—on the shoulder. With a brisk nod of his head, Thomas handed the man his stick, tapped the table, and gave the signature double-palms-up wave to the cameras and the crowd to show that he hadn't pocketed any chips (or any phone numbers).

Thomas left the table without so much as a word. Not even a wink. Was I not owed that? Just some trivial, flirtatious acknowledgment of our unspoken connection? The goddamn ring in his heart? Union rules and required breaks be damned. What we had was *special*.

I must've been visibly upset, because Angie gingerly placed her hand on my shoulder and whispered in my ear, "It's okay, Heather. He wasn't for you anyways. We'll get 'em next time, girl." As she squeezed my shoulder in a sign of sisterly support, I smiled ever so slightly. For as much as Angie's amateur matchmaking skills pale in comparison to the likes of her contemporaries', her instincts as a friend are second to none. For the rest of the night, she made me cry with laughter and never once offered up another dealer as a potential suitor. We had so much fun and won so much money that by the night's end, both Thomas and rotisserie chicken were all but a distant memory.

Men are a dime a dozen, but good friends are absolutely priceless. A shitty matchmaker perhaps, but a great gambler indeed, Angie knows that it's the biggest risks and the biggest gambles that result in the happiest endings in both love and craps.

Angie Katsanevas might be the worst wingman I've ever had, but she also tries to be my biggest cheerleader. She is a constant reminder to me that, when it comes to love—despite all of my hangups, anxieties, and inhibitions—it's always worth rolling the dice.

TWENTY-ONE

PUT ME IN NEUTRAL

I don't know why it always has to be about what we look like. It feels like this is true especially for women. How young, how old, how skinny, how fat, how glowed up, how glowed down, how natural, how fake. Women are constantly scrutinized, evaluated, and ranked based on their outward appearance. What we look like is always in the lead, and it drives the way we are received, supported, and celebrated.

I've spent the majority of my life trying not to let my appearance hold me back. Pushing past the prejudice and the stereotypes and the dismissive way we treat women who aren't conventionally attractive—overweight, bad hair, bad skin, bad shoes, small boobs, big boobs, saddle-bags, and saggy butts. Pretending not to see or feel the microaggressions, the tiny asides—the clear hierarchy that exists when you walk into a room and the beautiful women decide who is in charge. I tried to always lead with confidence and to never let the way people treated me

217

hold me back. But it didn't work. And sometimes, the tougher I acted, the harder they tried to slam me down.

I remember how in eleventh grade, in pottery class, I was getting teased by a senior boy who claimed I was in love with him.

"Don't flatter yourself," I said with an attitude.

He burst out laughing: "The only way I could flatter myself was if you sat on me."

All the students around us roared with laughter. I had asked for it, and he had gone for the low-hanging fruit of fat-shaming. And I felt it to my core. So much so that I'm writing about it right fucking now. I wish I remembered his name so that I could publicly shame him for being an asshole. But he wasn't the only one. It was grueling when I was younger. I was scared to ever admit to liking someone because I knew that just by mentioning a name, one of my prettier, thinner friends would suddenly be interested in the same person—even if it was just to subtly reinforce their dominance in the pretty-girl food chain.

On the night I met my ex-husband, it was clear that we had a connection, even though there were thinner, prettier girls in the room. My friend pulled me aside and reassured me, "Don't worry, I'm not into Billy." The unspoken reality was that she was letting me know that if she decided she *was* into him, there would be no question about who he would pick.

The saddest, worst part about it all is that I didn't even realize I wasn't the prettiest girl in the room until the world kept telling me. And sometimes I *still* refuse to accept it. I like my body and all the magnificent things it has done for me. The world told me that I should feel ashamed and embarrassed, or at least motivated to change it: to be smaller, to be softer, to be prettier. I never got a chance to try to be anything else, because I was already doing the math to become what I wasn't.

I remember in sixth grade dressing up for Halloween as a cheerleader. I had a vest and a pleated skirt, scrunchy socks, and my hair in a high pony. I probably still believed that I was going to be a cheerleader one day, or at least that it was within the realm of possibility. When I was looking at photos from that day with my mom, she paused on one photo of me, full body, facing the camera and smiling. She took her thumb and covered up my entire torso and showed it to me. "Look at how pretty your face and legs are," she explained. "Now, if you could just get rid of this . . ." and then she lifted her thumb, revealing my stomach in all its sixth-grade prepubescent glory. And the pretty face and legs she had mentioned vanished, swallowed up in the shame of the giant torso that connected my only redeeming parts.

In the church, we associate beauty with happiness and success. "Wickedness never was happiness" is a scripture from the Book of Mormon that we often quote as an admonition to avoid sin. But the undertone feels like, "Ugliness never was happiness . . ."

I grew up associating beauty with well-being, and well-being with well-living, not just in the church but everywhere. It must be a symptom of the society we live in. If you want to exist in a patriarchal culture, you have to be able to spend the local currency. And when the world is run by men, beauty seems to be what they're buying.

As much as I want to believe that beauty is in the eye of the beholder, too often it feels like the beholder can't see past an extra twenty pounds.

I think I hit max capacity for self-evaluation a few years ago, and it's just some sort of sick irony that I find myself now on television, where my face and body are broadcast to the world right when I'm ready to pack it all in and retire in a muumuu on an island somewhere.

I've spent my whole life apologizing for how I look and commiserating with those who found me unappealing. But the truth is, while I might've wanted to look different, I've always accepted what I looked like on the outside because I felt it was a tradeoff for who I was on the inside, and that part I never really wanted to change. And because of that, I found myself uniquely beautiful in my own way. I never extrapolated my inner- and outer-self because it all felt like a package deal. Sometimes, my confidence was confusing to people. They wondered how someone who looked like me could be so full of confidence. I chalked it all up to delusion—delusion about my appeal, and delusion about my own exaggerated abilities. But accepting what I look like doesn't mean that there aren't some days when I look at a photo of myself and want to take a hammer to my face. It is possible for self-esteem and self-loathing to simultaneously exist, and I'm here to prove it. In fact, you can argue that it's quite healthy to both admire what you love about yourself and wholly reject the things you wish you could change.

No one wants to be ugly, but I'm exhausted just trying NOT to be.

I know what it takes to put pretty on. I've built my livelihood on it. It's a mind-numbing, never-ending race to fight off all the natural ways our body wants to return to its resting state, i.e. ugly. The fucking GRIND of it all is exhausting. And expensive. And soul crushing. And even though we judge everyone's self-acceptance by their level of self-care, the beauty industry has made it increasingly harder and more expensive to accomplish it all.

Beauty Lab + Laser was the business I wanted to go to, but that didn't exist, so I decided to start it. I wanted to acknowledge the relentless and eternal beauty standards that we are judged by every day and to accommodate the people who wanted to look good but not waste their lives pursuing it. Because you could honestly dedicate your entire day every day to supposed self-care and still come up short. The manis/pedis, hair extensions, lash extensions, self-tan, deep condition, laser, Botox, mini lip plump, liquid nose job, tech neck, IPL, teeth whitening, teeth implanting, veneers, BBLs, lipo, Ozempic, and all the other GLP-1 medications that are all the rage. It's nothing new. I lived through Phen/Fen and lost the twenty pounds I'm so used to always carrying. I even tried to get it in Mexico illegally when the U.S. took it off the market. Yes, I was aware that it caused heart damage, but I didn't care. I didn't care as much as a meth addict doesn't care that smoking is ruining their teeth. Without it, I couldn't lose weight. And with it, I looked better enough to change the way people treated me.

Everything in the beauty world is based on the cycle of destruction, injury, and recovery. We injure the skin to force it to rejuvenate. We burn off spots that are too dark or uneven or hairy; we singe them with a fire-hot laser and then watch them crust and scab and heal and eventually slough off, revealing marginally newer, fresher traumatized skin and we call it self-care. We call it anti-aging. We call it beauty. We equate it with self-confidence and self-esteem and self-actualization. We say we're "putting ourselves back on the list." But if that's the cost of entry, take me off the list. Put the hot laser away, and put me in a dark, cool drawer and let me CHILL. OUT.

Of course, this seems absolutely ridiculous for me to say since my entire financial livelihood hinges on the fact that women are smart enough, rich enough, and brave enough to do this to themselves regularly. I see the women who come into Beauty Lab, and they are reliably there once a week. They spend tens of thousands of dollars, and they never miss a laser appointment or a lip injection. And they are beautiful. Stunning. Perfect even. It works if you work it. And I fucking admire them! I want to be like them. I want to care as much about what I look like as they do. Because they look better and they're treated better.

I know women that get their nails done twice a week, sitting for hours while they're hand-painted and bejeweled. They look forward to the hand massage. They inhale the acrylic dust with vigor. I meanwhile, can barely drag my craggy hands and toes in there every three weeks, and I dread every second of it. It hurts, it's uncomfortable, the chair is too low, the drill is too fast, and the conversation is too stunted. But it's not just nails. I hate getting my hair done too. When my ever-patient and always-kind hairstylist gently reminds me that it's time for a touch-up, I audibly groan. It's a fucking GRIND.

Ultimately, though, I keep up these appearances because I have to. If I step off the treadmill for one minute, I'll never be able to match the pace again, and I will be thrown out of the race entirely. The better you look, the better you are treated, and this is why my business thrives and why I put myself through the paces even though it's last on my priority list.

I've accepted that if the world sees you as beautiful, little else matters. Pretty privilege is the only thing that's acknowledged internationally in all circles, backgrounds, incomes, and industries. It is the universal, no-limit, Black Card access. And because we tell people that the way they look is their own personal choice, we pursue it like a rabbit at a greyhound race, instinctively knowing that we will never reach a resting state of pretty because it will always remain elusive.

While filming confessional interviews for *The Real Housewives of Salt Lake City*, I often joke that I'd rather do the interview in the shadows like a protected witness in a true crime documentary than be preened and primed with extra pounds of hair and makeup and squeezed into a cocktail dress. It's bad enough that we have to sit on a single stool for hours under camera-ready lights, but to do it all in full glam makes the whole process feel especially vulnerable.

When I look at my costars and friends, I love how beautiful they look, and I love that they relish their glam and their fashion. I am also always baffled at how they look so good, and I wonder if it requires the same Herculean effort that it requires for me.

Being on *Housewives* has thrown me into a world where I am judged constantly on my physical appearance right at the phase of life when I've finally gotten past all of the self-criticism and judgment. I want my body and my looks to be so transparent that people can just see through them, past them, and beyond them to the person that I am. And yet what I look like and what I weigh has always driven the narrative. But I don't want it to drive anything anymore. Please, just put me in neutral, and let's see where I end up. If I get uglier and fatter, I don't want people to assume it's because I'm depressed or unsuccessful. I might just be getting uglier and fatter because I'm getting older, and it's my goddamn right to age however I want. If I get prettier and thinner, it's probably because I have more money and time on my hands than ever before. It's not a transformation of my soul or of my self-care. It's just a transformation of how much cash and effort I'm willing to spend on my appearance.

I've been called a lot of different names over the course of my life, specifically over my five seasons on television. I've been called a size-fourteen Gucci, a manatee, Shrek. I've been called horrible things in private and public by my costars and the general public. But the second I began to lose weight, people started changing the things they said about me:

"You look great!"

"You look thin."

"Are you on Ozempic?"

For the first time, people wanted me to celebrate my looks instead of apologize for them, and it made me intensely uncomfortable. It was like I was being forced to swim in a swamp that I thought I had just climbed my way out of. Even after accomplishing things I never dreamed of, being on television, building a multimillion dollar company, writing a *New York Times* bestselling book, people seemed to act like losing weight was my greatest accomplishment to date. And while their attention and approval felt good, it also felt sad to me because it confirmed what I had always feared: being thin is more important than anything else. Nothing tastes as good as skinny feels, and nothing stings as much as realizing it.

I don't fault the world for marveling when people lose weight and change their bodies. It feels like some sort of miracle when it happens, so we naturally want to celebrate it. And I am marveling as much as anyone because I never believed it could happen to me. But as much as I'm amazed by it, it also confirms that my weight and appearance were always holding me back in other people's minds no matter how much I pretended they weren't.

Now that GLP-1 medications like Ozempic and Mounjaro, etc. are widely available and a proven solution, we are going to expect women to be skinny like never before. When I first went on weight-loss medication, it was a pretty slow-moving ship. I was pretty sure that it wasn't going to work, so sure in fact that I probably sabotaged myself for the first six months. It took me a very long time to see results. I was injecting once a week and losing about two pounds a month. But it was the first time in my life that the needle on the scale was trending down with what felt like very little effort.

That's not to say that going on weight-loss medication was easy. Because of the stigma, I almost didn't want it to work so that I could have a reason to stand with everyone on the sidelines that criticized the people who were using it like a crutch. And if it worked too well, I would be ashamed to have to admit to using it. I didn't want to have anything about myself that I'd have to hide. Luckily, the reoccurring theme in my life appeared again: I fell somewhere in the middle. The Semaglutide was working, but it was working very slowly. So, as the months ticked by with "illicit" weight loss noticeable only to me, I found myself caught, once again, in the "in-between."

The weight loss was so gradual that, when the number finally reached twenty-five pounds, it was the first time the change was noticeable, so people assumed I had lost it all overnight. And the more attention I got from it, the worse I felt about how I looked before. I've been thin and I've been fat, and the only thing that really changes is the way people treat me. I feel the same on the inside—I have the same ambition, the same anxieties, the same passions, the same fears. My pant size might get smaller, but none of my other problems ever shrink accordingly.

It shouldn't require so much work to feel good about ourselves.

It shouldn't require drinking so much water, feeling so much hunger, sweating through so much miserable exercise, paying thousands and thousands of dollars in appointments and treatments. I don't want to go to bed hungry. I don't want to waste the precious real estate in my brain on calories-in, calories-out, and counting the grams of fat in my eggs Benedict. I've never been good with numbers anyway. And when it comes down to losing weight, numbers are all that matters.

My life is immeasurably better when I'm eating exactly what I want to eat, and when I'm indulging, hanging out, and not beating myself up over my lack of activity or my lack of restraint. It's when I start depriving myself, when I go to bed hungry and sweat at the gym daily, that I feel the most miserable. But the world would interpret this routine as an indication of self-love when it feels like self-loathing. I promise you, when I love myself the most, I'm eating and laughing and lazing around with my friends. I don't reward myself with a trip to the gym or a hike up the canyon; I reward myself with baggy sweats, a lot of treats, and streaming services on every channel.

I don't see why I can't just sleep and stream season after season of *Succession* and still look as good as I feel after a fifteen-episode binge. I'm tired of operating on hyperdrive. Just let me shift down a few gears and put me in neutral. Let me cruise. Isn't that what we all deserve? A bit of body neutrality?

I'll take myself out of the "in-between" and keep myself coasting in neutral.

TWENTY-TWO

RECEIPTS! PROOF! TIMELINE! SCREENSHOTS!

knew I had to confront her, but I didn't know when or how. That fucking bitch! *"How could she do this to us?"*

This was a moment of sheer rage, but also of heartbreak. It wasn't your typical *Housewives*-caliber betrayal; this thing had LAYERS. WAS Monica the world's best con artist? HAD she actually hacked *Housewives*? WAS she planted by production? It was my own, "How could you do this to me ... question mark," moment just like Countess Luann in her Miami hotel room.

The way the story unfolded in real life was much like it happened on television, only more dramatic and unbelievable with a much longer timeline. Monica Darnell-Fowler-Dalgado-Garcia had cracked the *Housewives* code. Based on the receipts, she had plotted and schemed and weaseled her way onto the show under the falsest of pretenses and in the creepiest of ways. She was the *wrong* kind of crazy. We had an imposter among us, and I wasn't even sure there was anything we could do about it. But the receipts, the proof, and the screenshots could not be ignored.

This crisis would eventually become the epic season 4 finale episode of *The Real Housewives of Salt Lake City*. The episode that turned *Housewives* fans on their heads. The most watched episode in the history of the show, and the pop-culture zenith that was quoted in Congress, became a Broadway mashup sensation, and was heralded at the Academy Awards by Oscar-winner Jennifer Lawrence herself. Our faces and story were plastered across the internet, receiving features in *Vulture*, *Variety*, and *Time*, while *Entertainment Weekly* dubbed the final reveal the "biggest bomb in franchise history." More than that though, it was a story about friendship. We were a group of friends who, when tested, looked beyond our own petty drama and, for the first time, let the problem pull us together instead of tear us apart. However, when the events of that now-celebrated episode occurred during a stormy night on the island of Bermuda, none of us were imagining what it would become; we were too busy surviving it.

How *had* this happened? To understand, we have to go back to the beginning. We have to examine the *"Receipts! Proof! Timeline! Screenshots!"* And even then, we may never understand *FUCKING EVERYTHING!*

RECEIPTS!

In *Silence of the Lambs*, Hannibal Lechter explains to the novice FBI agent Clarice Starling that most serial killers don't start out by killing; they start out by *coveting*. And they covet what they see: *"We begin by coveting what we see every day. Don't you feel eyes moving over your body, Clarice? And don't your eyes seek out the things you want?"*

Monica was not a serial killer, far from it, but, in some ways, she wasn't that different from Buffalo Bill. She started out by coveting, and, as the subject of her obsession, *Real Housewives* everywhere weren't sure if she wanted to "be us, or skin us and wear us like last year's Versace."

Monica was obsessed with *The Real Housewives*. But more than just *The Real Housewives*, she seemed to be obsessed with FAME. In her 1,200-square-foot rambler in Kaysville, Utah, overflowing with four kids and a giant labrador retriever, no one would fault her for wanting to escape. And it's easy to escape into the opulence of *Housewives*. It's why many love to watch, and it's one reason why the franchise is so far-reaching. For Monica, however, it landed a little differently. What she watched, she wanted. And she couldn't go about her normal life without thinking about it.

She had fantasies about being famous. Being an influencer. Being riiiich. She gushed about it in voice recordings, talking about showing up at her friends' houses with a brand-new car with a "motherfuck-ing" bow on it and making dinner reservations on the "Eiffel fucking Tower": *"If one of us gets rich first, No! WHEN one of us gets rich first, whoever gets rich first. Mmmmmmmkay? Everyone's coming with ME. I mean like, you guys pack your bags. We leave tomorrow to fucking go shopping in gay Par-ee bitches. Okay? That's legit how rich I want to be. And for sure, there's a fourth, fifth, sixth, seventh, eighth, ninth, tenth, eleventh, twelfth kind of rich honey, one hundy percent. You bet."*

While she craved the good life, she confessed to friends that her lack of wealth and checkered past would keep her from ever being on TV. She was still recovering from the aftermath of her scandalous divorce and was entering a new chapter of her life. She had been caught sleeping with her brother-in-law, and the entire family discovered that the two had been having an affair right underneath their noses for over a year and a half. She had been excommunicated from the church and ultimately gotten divorced. But she explained that through sincere repentance and a lot of hard work, she recommitted herself to the church, got rebaptized, and reconciled with her ex-husband. They remarried and shortly thereafter added two new babies to their brood. She longed to be like the Mormon "mommy influencers" she followed on Instagram. And she worked hard at it. But it wasn't easy with four kids, two under two, and a lifestyle that, no matter how she styled it, couldn't keep up with the Joneses. But she was determined. And she was crafty. And she didn't take no for an answer.

It all started on Instagram. Her IG profile was @westleemae. She described herself as an active member of the LDS church. A married, stay-at-home mom of four little girls with dreams of building a cottage-industry baby blanket business out of her living room. She dressed modestly and went to church every Sunday. She posted family pics with her now-remarried-to ex-husband, and she tried to network with every local blogger that would have her. She built relationships on what she thought they might have in common: flat belly tea, Stanley cups, and Target hauls.

When the cast of season 1 of *The Real Housewives of Salt Lake City* was officially announced, she began networking immediately. She became a customer of my business, Beauty Lab + Laser, and booked as many services as she could afford. She talked about reaching out to Whitney Rose's company to inquire about being an ambassador for her newly launched skincare line. She reached out to Lisa Barlow, gushing over her VIDA tequila and style. And she messaged Meredith Marks with effusive fervor hoping to make an impression. No one took her up on her offers of assistance, except for Jen.

Jen Shah was a Real Housewife with an explosive Machiavellian personality that stole America's attention the second she burst onto the screen. She had taken to fledgling celebrity life with bombastic flair and hired as many assistants as she could. The term "hired" might be a little misleading, because it was rumored that none of the assistants were ever paid or compensated in any significant way. But nonetheless, she began to build an entourage, and Monica, née Westleemae, was pining to be a part of it.

Westleemae's constant social-media presence kept her connected to Jen on Instagram, but she was finding it difficult to meet her in person. Miraculously, Monica suddenly had what appeared to be a stroke of luck. In preparation for filming, Jen went on Thumbtack in search of a handyman to build an IKEA closet in her Park City rental house. While searching for the right guy for the job, she stumbled on Monica's husband. He had listed the exact Thumbtack skills she was looking for. He was the perfect choice—the only choice. This was Monica's big break. She finally had an "in" with Jen Shah. She claimed that she had no idea who Jen Shah was when he took the job, but she magically showed up at Jen's house, accompanying him on his first day of work. It quickly became clear that Monica was planning on staying around: "He'll build your closet, and I'll be your best friend!" If the closet didn't work out, she'd at least get to check out where Jen lived and hopefully make enough of a connection to get a photo for her feed.

Joining the entourage wasn't as tough a gig as Monica imagined. Jen had a nose for exploitable desperation and drama, and Monica reeked of both. Jen sniffed her out immediately and welcomed her with open arms.

This was our first introduction to Monica: as a mom named West-leemae in 2020, months before the first episode of *The Real Housewives of Salt Lake City* had even aired. Angie Katsenevas was the first cast member outside of Jen to meet Westleemae in person. It was on set for a video Jen wanted to make for Instagram. After meeting Angie that day, Monica immediately went home and liked twenty of her pictures on Instagram. Angie thought it was weird.

Lisa Barlow was the next one to meet her and it was at the Salt Lake City airport on her way to film the season 1 reunion. Jen had forgotten some essential reunion props and arranged for Monica to drop them off so that Lisa could bring them to her in New York. As she was checking her bags, Lisa was approached by what she described as a "curvy, blonde, disheveled mom with her hair in a banana clip that looked like she hadn't showered in days." "I never would have recognized her!" she recollected. She was wearing bad jeans and cheap flip-flops even though it was January and there was snow on the ground. It was Monica/Westleemae, and she was beyond excited to finally get to see Lisa in the flesh after months of eavesdropping on her conversations with Jen.

She appeared embarrassed that Jen hadn't included her on the trip to NYC, instead leaving her to stay home and run lowly errands. Jen had never considered taking Monica in the first place. She had four kids at home, including a two-year-old and a baby, and she was someone Jen felt obligated to help, not actually employ. Monica made it clear that she didn't like being treated like an assistant, and I'm sure it must've felt especially humiliating to be chasing through the airport for a trip she wasn't invited to be on in order to assure that Jen's "SHADY" fan made it into Lisa's designer carry-on.

By the time she got home from the airport she was licking her wounds and psyching herself back up: *"Yes, bitch. Yes, yes, motherfuck-*

ing yes. Fucking Kim Kardashian was a fucking assistant and look at that bitch now. I can fully admit that the whole reason why I was an assistant and putting up with that shit was as a stepping stone, as a learning experience, only to like, proceed myself." Her aspiration in life was not to wipe Jen Shah's "motherfucking ass." The sting of being left behind and excluded from the reunion wasn't fading. It was the beginning of the end of their relationship.

To Monica, Jen was more than just her celebrity crush, she also seemed to be an easy mark—she described her as a heavy drinker, prone to blackouts, with discretionary cash and discretionary assistants. Someone who was casual about her cash and credit card numbers. She complained that Jen drank two bottles of tequila a day and that she was constantly so drunk "she didn't know what the fuck she was doing." She had never been around booze or bling like Jen's before, and she smelled opportunity. She was being treated like an employee, but she wasn't being paid for any of her time, so she played the role of a friend and leaned into Jen's sympathies. She'd get cash handouts when she could. She would call Jen crying and complain about her car payment being due, "is there any way you could possibly help?" The car dealership had the ability to remotely shut her car off if the payments were missed and she needed to be able to take the girls to school. Jen would step in and pay the bill and Monica would promise to work it off. She began bringing her children over to Jen's house with her and she claimed that the Shahs were overly generous. Taking her kids in as their own, buying them clothes and treats whenever they could. A check here, a bill paid there. Jen was sure that Monica would work everything off and Monica was sure that she would never have to.

They were both wrong.

Jen expressed concern behind Monica's back. She felt bad for her kids, and she wanted to help. Monica was eager to let her. "If she's offering, I'm accepting!" She bragged about Jen's money in text messages to friends, oohing and aahing over her disregard for budgets, and her love for designer labels and department-store makeup.

Her husband, as the handyman, had been her initial entrance into Jen's world. But now that she felt cemented in Jen's circle, his presence grew to be a liability. He was a witness to how much time Monica spent and how little money she actually got. In his opinion, this wasn't a friendship OR a job. It was bullshit, and he didn't like it. Monica couldn't have cared less. When he brought it up, she complained about their lack of finances and threatened to *"divorce his ass . . . again."* The honeymoon phase of their vow renewal and new babies was over. He wasn't making enough money, and the pressure from Monica was mounting. She had divorced him once before, and he had shown up on her doorstep every day until she took him back. She knew *he* wasn't going anywhere, but if her friendship with Jen panned out the way she planned, she *might* be. She encouraged him to take a job selling solar panels in North Carolina in an effort to send money back home. "We're better when we're apart," she promised him. He reluctantly agreed.

With her hubby's watchful eye no longer looming above her, Monica moved things up a notch. Now it was easier for her to slip away, sleep over at Jen's house or be available on a moment's notice. If Jen needed a ride home at 3:00 in the morning, Monica would drop everything to get her, leaving her kids under the care of her oldest. It wasn't a big deal. By then, her daughter had grown accustomed to being the one in charge. She was responsible and wise beyond her years. She woke up early every day, made breakfast for her younger siblings, and drove them to school while Monica slept in, exhausted by her late-night escapades. Her mom later complained on Twitter that this behavior was nothing new. Monica had been tasking her oldest with parenting duties for years, and Twitter was her favorite place to publicly complain about it.

But the demands from Jen were slowly increasing, and the charm and appreciation she usually felt was wearing thin. By the time Monica was running through the airport to meet up with Lisa, she was finally over it. The lunches and shopping and hand-me-down bags weren't enough to make up for the amount of time she was spending away from her own life. She deserved compensation. She stopped relying on sad stories to get money from Jen and instead charted her hours and asked for an actual paycheck. And the pushier she got, the more Jen pulled away. Jen was onto her.

She stopped including her on the Shah Squad group texts and rarely responded to her calls or text messages. The sudden silence was deafening and Monica began to spiral. Did Jen need her to drop by today? "What's the plan? I'm available!" Nothing seemed to work. This added insult to injury. She wasn't getting paid and now she was definitely getting ghosted. Monica was in a tailspin. Where had all the sympathy for her and her family gone? Weren't they *friends*? How could you do this to me . . . question mark.

In a final Hail Mary attempt for a handout she reached out to Jen's husband Sharrieff. Supposedly, they agreed to meet up in the parking lot of a gas station and, according to Monica, the exchange quickly turned romantic. She claims he tried to kiss her, but she pushed him off, saying, "We can't." Sharrieff got out of the car and immediately left. But no one believed her. She was getting desperate and was known for cranking up the delusion when cornered. By all accounts, she had been pining for

Sharrieff from the moment she met him, and this was one of her absurd fantasies. Still, she swore that they had kissed, but nothing more had happened between them after that night. She was notoriously full of lies.

With Sharrieff unable to help her, Monica was being forced to accept that her run with the Shahs was over. Like with any good con, you need to know when the gig is up and she knew it. Her husband was living across state lines, her baby blanket business was dwindling, and Jen was pulling the plug on their "friendship" all before filming for season 2 even began. She was beside herself with rage, like a knockoff Regina George realizing she'd been eating high-calorie Kalteen bars instead of diet meal replacements. She was angry—spitting and wailing and gnashing-of-teeth angry—and she wasn't going to take it lying down.

She began hatching her revenge. She had had enough of watching Jen's popularity grow while she was being depleted. By now, Jen's presence on the show and on social media had made her a bona fide villain with influence and fame, and she wasn't sharing any of it with Monica. If she wasn't going to have the perks of being famous, then Jen wasn't either. She decided to expose her. She would take Jen Shah down and make her suffer while she did it.

It was in this fit of anger that Reality Von Tease was born.

PROOF!

Monica already had the content she knew she needed. She had been stockpiling hidden videos of Jen for months before Jen cut off all contact.

As the helpful friend/assistant, she had been the one to convince Jen that she needed security cameras in her house. Monica set up the appointments, the access emails, and all the passwords. She staged fights with Jen in areas where she knew there were security cameras, then she'd screen record the footage and store it away for the day she would need it. She made sure that the camera feeds came to her phone so that when she wasn't there, she could watch and listen to the Shahs around the clock. Forget the comparison to Buffalo Bill in *Silence of the Lambs*. She had graduated from just coveting into absolutely obsessing. She went full *Baby Reindeer*.

Once it became clear that Jen was done with her, she reached out to other disgruntled former assistants and assembled a team. It was a group of five who shared very little in common other than an enemy. But for Monica, that was enough for now. She was used to having disposable friends, and she needed them to share this secret so the culpability wouldn't be hers alone. They sat around a table and talked about how they could expose Jen without exposing themselves. Monica took the lead. She decided to leak a video where Jen had been caught screaming. She knew they needed it to be seen by the right influencers in order to get traction. Monica began by writing down every Bravo account she could think of on a single piece of paper. This would be her hit list, the bloggers she would tag in every post in order to go viral. They numbered over seventy-eight names, and Monica knew most of them by heart. At the top of the list were the IG profiles of the entire cast of *Salt Lake City*.

Reality Von Tease was launched. Her Instagram profile picture was a photo of the masked burlesque dancer, Dita Von Teese, and the bio read: *"Reality Von (Tea)se—Your local RHOSLC hot tea hoe. For entertainment purposes ONLY."* This was not Monica's first burner account—it was reportedly one of many—but it was the first one that had any actual tea to drop, thanks to Jen's celebrity and the security cameras she had set up inside the house. The first video depicted Jen in a velvet floral Versace blazer screaming across a bar top in her kitchen at two people off camera. She hurls a slew of obscenities at them and then storms off, throwing something in their direction as she leaves. Monica would later refer to this as "chili bowl night."

"SHOCKING LEAKED FOOTAGE OF JEN SHAH ABUSING HER EMPLOYEES," she alleged in the caption, and she tagged everyone on her list. The post immediately blew up. The rush of the attention and audience filled Monica with a purpose and sensation she hadn't experienced before. Was this what it felt like to be famous? She mused with her co-conspirators, "I think I found my calling." She loved the attention, and she wanted more.

A group text chain shows just how closely she monitored every view, like, and comment. *"OMG OMG!"* she texted in all caps. *"ZADDY ANDY SAW MY POST!! Hi bebe!"* Attached was a screenshot of her story views with the profile @bravoandy circled in red. She crowed about the account's success in voice memos and videos, detailing every save, share, and comment. When Bravo influencers viewed her content but failed to repost or share it, she was furious, calling them "fuck face stanky bitches" and threatening to unfollow their accounts if they didn't start to reciprocate.

As Reality Von Tease, she felt more like Jen Shah than ever, and she reportedly delighted in giving Jen a taste of her own medicine online.

When Reality Von Teases's first video hit the internet, I, like my castmates, was shocked. Not just by what Jen was doing—by now, both the cast and the viewing audience had seen behavior like this from Jen before—but by the way the video was filmed and leaked. It felt like an absolute invasion of privacy from someone clearly on the inside, and it was unsettling. Who had betrayed her? Filming for season 2 had already begun and none of us really remembered Westleemae/Monica, let alone suspected her to be the culprit.

Within days of the first post, a cease and desist was sent from Jen's attorney regarding violations of Monica's nondisclosure agreement, specifically citing Reality Von Tease. It was a fishing expedition on Jen's part, and she never told any of us about it. By now, the Shahs had realized that Monica was the one who had set up their security feed, which meant that, even if she wasn't the one actually posting on Reality Von Tease, she was at the very least providing the content. They tried to reset the password and an alert came through to Monica's phone. She immediately freaked out in the group chat, lamenting not that she might be caught, but that she would be cut off from the cameras, and more importantly, cut off from her daily fix of watching Jen, her eternal muse.

Regardless of her bravado, the cease and desist got her attention. She toyed with the idea of shutting the page down, but she didn't want to give it up. They were hot on her trail, and she knew that her access to the security cameras made her vulnerable. When her friends tried to convince her that she had covered her tracks, she still wasn't reassured: *"Ok, I agree with you on a lot of that except for the cameras. That was all me. Like, I'm the one that brought it up; I'm the one that forced it; I'm the one that scheduled it. She never even talked about that. Like, that was literally all me."*

She wanted to be sure she couldn't get sued so she reached out to "a friend's uncle who was also an attorney," and decided to add "allegedly" to all the posts. And then, emboldened by her increasing followers, she convinced herself that she wasn't doing anything wrong: "None of that shit was illegally obtained. Thank you next . . ." She told herself that because she was the only one with access to the security footage, she had legal rights to everything they recorded. She referred to them as "my cameras" and she was glued to everything they filmed. She dared anyone to tell her otherwise. "People are so fucking stupid. Where? Why? What do they even need for proof? No proof of anything bitch. I dropped those recordings. What are you going to do about it? People are idiots."

Reality Von Tease began posting with increased venom for all things *Housewives* and Jen Shah. Then, when she thought more leaked video and audio recordings would take down Jen, the federal government swooped in and said to Reality Von Tease, "hold my beer." Jen Shah was arrested. A SWAT team of heavily armed officers, Homeland Security, and FBI agents swarmed the parking lot of Beauty Lab + Laser while we were filming for season 2. The officers were looking for Jen, and the cameras caught every moment. Jen had fled the scene just before they arrived, and she was arrested shortly thereafter on the shoulder of a local highway. A few minutes later, she was charged with conspiracy to commit wire fraud and money laundering. Monica couldn't believe her luck, and the runway for her trolling opened wide.

"SHE IS GOING TO PRISON BITCH!!!!!!! Clinkety Clinkety Clink! I'M FUCKING DYIIIIIIINNNNNGGG! SHE IS FUCKKKKKKKED. CLANK CLANK!" The group chat lit up! Reality Von Tease began gathering information and posting three, four, sometimes five times a day on her feed, and nine, ten, sometimes eleven times on her story, tagging everyone on the *Salt Lake City* cast individually. Instagram was on fire, and Monica's content coffers were full. Every meme, article, gif, and reel was repurposed for Reality Von Tease, and her fix had never been stronger. Her dream of being adjacent to Jen faded. Who needs *Housewives* when you have the entire internet?

She needed to find more ways to be involved, so she reached out to the investigators assigned to Jen's case and offered up her testimony. Maybe she could be of help? After all, she had worked for Jen and claimed she witnessed her crimes. Every time she thought of something suspicious, she sent an email, and complained when they were slow to contact her and respond: *"Hi there. I'm sure you are very busy, and I had (sp) emailed you several times in regards to information about the Jen Shah case. I have been told that the assistant has been storing things for her at his home, several bags full of things. He is holding them for her so that they don't get taken. I was told this at the time that I emailed you the first time. I don't know if he still has them at his home or not, but he has been the one holding on to or moving these bags for her. Thank you, Monica."*

The investigators set up a video conference with their victim witness coordinator, and Monica bragged about how excited she was to meet with them. "The second I heard they were looking for information I beep beep boop brillllllllllll!" she gushed. "I called up that number so fast! Um yessss, the bitch did it! And I'm happy to say she did it and that I witnessed all of it. The bitch fucking did it!"

But it was all a lie. She hadn't witnessed anything substantive. The feds weren't concerned about how Jen had hurt Monica's feelings and cut her off; they were concerned with how she had ripped off the elderly. And Jen had never trusted Monica on that level. The detectives responded politely to her relentless inquiries: "Received and thank you, please send no more texts in this regard." They suggested she move on with her life and try to heal. They would reach out if they needed her.

But Monica doubled down. Now that she had been cut off from the cameras, she had no idea what Jen was up to and it drove her crazy. She was prohibited from entering Jen's gated community in Park City, so she asked her husband to help her get past security. He used his handyman credentials from the closet building gig to get another contractor's pass, and Monica made a video fanning herself with the yellow placard, bragging, "Ohhhhh. Look what I got! A Promontory Pass? Whaaaaaaaat? Cuz a bitch doesn't take no for an answer! MUAHAHAHA!"

They drove immediately past the gate and began recording their attack. Her husband held an open bottle in his hand, and she filmed him as he drove through the winding streets of the neighborhood, marveling at all the big houses. The camera bounced back between him and the road ahead. He was clearly her unwilling accomplice and was never accused of having the same obsession or intentions as Monica. But the tragedy of the scene is hard to miss, and it's easy to feel sorry for both of them. You can see that the windshield is cracked in three different directions, and that the sun-faded dashboard is dusty and littered with trash. It's the perfect setting for a horror movie. And then, Monica begins to sing loudly, off-key, *The* OC theme song, "California," but she substitutes the original lyrics with the name of Jen's gated community: "Promontory, here we come. Right back where we started from, Promontory!" The demented tone in her voice is hard to contain. She appears to be a woman on a mission. As they make the turn to Jen's house, her husband threatens to honk and Monica squeals, "Don't you DARE! Seriously! I don't need a restraining order for stalking!" She stops filming briefly to take more pictures and then records the house as he slowly drives away, "Rot in prison, bitch!"

Once Jen moved out of the gated neighborhood, it became much easier for Monica to do what can only be described as FBI level surveillance. She spent hours researching where Jen had moved and posted photos of her moving truck, her address, and the new rent she was paying based on what she found on Zillow: "You guys…the rent is $5,000! And she can't pay us what she owes? We should sue her!"

She spent the next few months driving by Jen's house multiple times a day hoping to catch a glimpse of Jen or Coach Shah, or anyone and anything that she could use as content. She repeatedly begged in the group chat for info on where the other Housewives lived: *"Bitch!! We're in Holladay!!! What's Heather's address??? Where does she live? We just want to see it!!"*

She ventured out on her drive-bys daily: "I'm in the hood, bitch. These houses are boujie as FUCKKKKKK. I need to make friends with someone here so that I can be like, 'I'm just visiting my friend. Fuck you,' if she sees me." She gave a play-by-play of her every move in a whispered, maniacal voice, "Okay, holy fucking shit, you guys, I'm almost on the street. I'm so scared. Please don't be here"—even though it was obvious that she wanted her to be.

Her obsession had turned dark, and what started out as an airing of grievances had grown stale. Most of her one-time allies had moved on from Reality Von Tease and encouraged her to do the same: "No reason to keep it going." Jen's fame and success on the show were unaffected by her constant trolling and it was taking up more time than anyone felt comfortable with.

But Monica had fully embodied her role as Reality Von Tease by now, and she refused to let go. It wasn't so much about ruining Jen anymore as it was about being a part of the action and the rush she felt from the social-media frenzy. The attention she got made her feel powerful. It made her feel alive: "I honestly feel like my hatred for Jen is curing my depression. LOLZ!"

She filmed herself sitting in the car outside Jen's house, the camera lens focused on any observable motion. She experimented with disguises and bought tiny binoculars. Sometimes, when she passed her house, she could see Jen in the upstairs window, and she'd get especially excited, turning around to drive by again and snap a picture of the shadowy figure. She'd hyperventilate with joy and report back to the group chat, circling the picture in red and writing, "JEN?" When she saw her, she recorded herself screaming and acting like a crazed 1960s teenager catching a glimpse of The Beatles.

TIMELINE!

November 2019: Bravo announces *The Real Housewives of Salt Lake City*.

January 2020: Monica meets Jen.

February 2021: Reality Von Tease is launched on Instagram.

March 2021: Jen Shah is arrested and charged with conspiracy to commit wire fraud and money laundering.

February 2023: Filming for season 4 of *The Real Housewives of Salt Lake City* begins, and Monica Garcia is a part of the cast.

January 2024: The season 4 finale airs and Monica is exposed as Reality Von Tease.

When Episode 10 of season 2 aired featuring Jen's arrest, Monica bragged about how she appeared on the security footage in Meredith's store: "BITCH THAT WAS ME!" She accused Jen of being too drunk to remember the details from the scene. "She didn't even realize she bought me the other clutch!" she laughed. She had finally made it on the TV screen, and even though she was wearing a COVID mask and the scene was in black-and-white, she felt like a superstar. Her desire to be just like Jen was stronger than ever.

When casting directors posted that they were looking for new Housewives for season 3, she lost her mind, confiding to her friends, "OMGGGGGGG! THIS CAN'T BE REAL?" But the wheels were already turning: *"Listen you guys, at the end of the day, what I really want is to be a STAR, bitch! HAHAHA."*

Now, perhaps for the first time, she felt like she knew how to do it. She had studied Jen, copied Jen, emulated everything about Jen, but she had never tried to be Jen. With the success of Reality Von Tease, it's not hard to believe that she felt empowered enough to do it. She was a quick learner, and time spent in the DMs bonding with every Bravo account on Instagram had given her a crash course on what worked and what got you canceled as a Housewife. She knew what the audience wanted and how to give it to them. The second she felt like she had the perfect formula for succeeding on reality TV, her authenticity went out the window.

She started with her name. She needed to come up with something new, something different. She switched her IG name from @westleemae to @monicanikidalgado. She liked it. She liked how Niki sounded young and cool and Dalgado sounded just exotic enough.

A few people gave her pushback: "Why are you changing your name? Are you getting divorced?" There was no rhyme nor reason behind it. At the time, she was still married, and the name seemingly had no familial significance or origin. She admitted to her closest friends that she wanted a fresh start, a clean slate and a new identity.

She brushed off most of the criticism, but one comment stuck: "Dalgado? What's Dalgado? Where is that name from?"

In her haste she hadn't done enough research. Delgado was a very common last name around the world, but DALGADO, for the most part, didn't exist. She had spelled it wrong. It was a vulnerability she couldn't risk. So, she switched it again, this time to the fail-safe Garcia. There was no chance of spelling *that* wrong.

Gone were the descriptors she had always gone by: Mormon, married, wannabe influencer. She transformed overnight into a person who could easily become a reality TV star. She had a cloudy history, a CVS receipt–long list of creditors and unpaid traffic violations, plus there was the whole mess of the affair with her brother-in-law that she was hoping a name change might avoid. Then, there was the matter of her business. With unfulfilled baby blanket orders pending and disgruntled vendors demanding payment, she needed to change the name of that as well: Westleemae Blankets became La Brea Baby (supposedly named after one of her favorite places to visit in California), and the new website banner stated that it was owned and operated by never-heard-of-her-before-now, Monica Garcia.

For her casting interview, Monica slicked her hair back and borrowed a dark brunette wig from a friend. She wore giant hoop earrings and a white off-the-shoulder ruffled blouse. "Okayyyy. This is the vibe," she says. She pans the camera and gestures to the backdrop she's constructed in her bedroom: a jute macrame garland draped along the headboard with a round raffia mirror balanced against the wall above her head. *"Locat-sh-i-ohn,"* she explains with a flick of her wrist. Off camera, someone makes a noise. Monica stops her demonstration abruptly, looks away, and screams, "SHUT UP!" Then returns her gaze to the camera and smiles.

She was unhinged, she was curated, she was confident. She was what she thought was the perfect formula.

In her submission email she described herself as a feisty excommunicated Latina. She left out the fact that she had been re-baptized and was still attending church. "You need me on the show immediately!" she claimed. She dyed her blond hair back to dark and started posing under her new identity, hoping it was more than just her link to Jen that made her interesting.

When the casting interviews started, she realized it was harder than she thought to keep her multiple identities contained, "I wish I could apply as Reality Von Tease," she joked. "She has more followers than me. Muahahahahaha!"

As meetings with casting progressed, they asked her directly if she would be willing to come on the show as Jen's friend. Whaaaat?! Reality Von Tease and Jen Shah breaking bread together? If only they knew her true identity! She was confident they would never figure it out, and even if they did, they would never be able to prove it. But still, she was nervous that someone would rat her out. If Bravo found out what she was up to, she talked about how they wouldn't touch her with a ten-foot pole. And it worried her. But not enough to tell the truth or refuse to film with Jen. "Whatever it takes," she replied. "I'm your girl."

By now, production was up and running on season 3 and Jen, despite her pending federal charges, was filming daily. They suggested Monica join her in an upcoming scene as a friend.

"Are you still in touch with Jen?" they asked.

"Sadly, no," she replied, and confessed that Jen had blocked her.

They asked if she'd be willing to film with her if they arranged it, and she readily agreed. She even offered to reach out to Jen herself if they thought it would help? She knew Jen had suspected her of leaking the footage to Reality Von Tease but she was pretty confident that Jen didn't believe she was *actually* Reality Von Tease. With a potential prison sentence looming, it seemed obvious to everyone Jen was focused on bigger things now, and a random troll account that was once a big deal was dwarfed in comparison to the criminal charges she was facing.

Monica was seemingly willing to forgive and move on so long as it got her one step closer to stardom. It seemed like she was more open to shutting down Reality Von Tease now that it was in exchange for something bigger, but she kept it going, presumably in order to hang on to it through Jen's trial which would guarantee her endless content and engagement with her followers. She confessed that she would miss the power she felt, but she didn't want to risk it. Besides she had her other burner accounts to play with that weren't on Jen's radar. She was resolved. If casting wanted her to be Jen's friend, she'd be the best goddamn friend possible. It was *Housewives* or nothing.

An initial meeting was set. Jen and Monica met up at Red Iguana in downtown Salt Lake City and shared enough margaritas to make peace; and for Monica they may as well have achieved world peace because Jen agreed to film with her. It was all happening!

Then, within a few hours, a major setback. Jen changed her mind; she revoked the deal to film with her and Monica was out. No one is sure what caused the abrupt change, but the word on the curb is that Sharrieff found out about their reconciliation and forbade the two women from filming together. Monica was incensed!

Making peace was now long forgotten, and she set out to retaliate. Monica called and informed the officials assigned to Jen's case that she had witnessed Jen drinking alcohol and was "pretty sure" that it was a violation of her bond agreement. Production and the feds were confused by her story. How could someone pretending to be Jen's friend also be trying to get her arrested? Monica's chance at a guest appearance with or without Jen Shah for season 3 disappeared entirely. She was absolutely despondent.

"Don't worry," the casting department reassured her. "For some women, it takes three or four years of applying before they make it. Don't give up yet."

"Oh, girl. I have been struggling with this shit! I fucking love you. Thank you. Thank you for the freaking sweetest and kindest words. And I believe them—I'll make it one day—which is the most important part," she responded.

But she didn't really believe them. She was scared she had blown it, and her one chance to get on the show, as Jen's friend, would be gone once Jen went to prison. To come so close and then lose it was an injustice she couldn't stand.

As her resentment grew, so did her number of troll accounts and hateful posts. She expanded her target to all Housewives, with a special focus on SLC. "TRASH BUCKET BITCH," she wrote under a photo of Whitney Rose. "FAKEST ON THE CAST," under a photo of Meredith Marks. "UGLIEST KISSY FACE EVER," on a glamor shot of Lisa Barlow. "NOT ONE POC," she wrote under a photo of me on a girls' trip. She posted the footage of Jen's arrest over and over and over again tagging every Housewife and Housewife-adjacent account she could, often reaching the limit per post: *"OLD PEOPLE EVERYWHERE CELEBRATING YOUR A$$ GETTING ARRESTED!"*

Jen's trial date was looming. Now, with renewed fervor, the disgruntled Reality Von Tease was planning on using every detail of Jen's court appearances to skyrocket with content. She wanted to go to NYC to be in the courtroom, but she couldn't afford the ticket, and it was rumored that she asked the detectives directly if they would fly her out. "Who is this?" they responded. "Please do not contact us further."

Throughout season 3, Jen continued to proclaim her innocence, and production filmed with her up until the night before her trial. Then, she shocked everyone by admitting guilt for the very first time and striking a plea deal her first morning in court, minutes before the judge could even call a single witness. *"CLINK CLINK,"* Monica rejoiced on the blog. She sent out a photo of me, Meredith Marks, and Jen Shah in NYC: *"FUCKING PIECES OF SHIT."*

Jen was facing up to fifty years for her crimes, but her plea deal ensured that she would spend less than ten in prison. She was ultimately sentenced to six and a half. Monica had more than one reason to rejoice at the sentence. With Jen away for the foreseeable future, did that mean there was a spot available on the cast? She began texting the casting department immediately.

When her 2004 Acura MDX got repossessed for lack of payment, she begged her mom to take out an auto loan so she could get a new car in order to impress casting. She convinced her to buy a used Range Rover and got it wrapped to look as much like Lisa Barlow's as possible.

Her mom protested and told her to stop pining after *Housewives*. She begged her to get a real job, encouraging her to put her social-media skills to work and to take on clients or build web pages. Why waste your talent on trolling? Reality Von Tease only had a few thousand followers and she wasn't monetizing any of it. "I don't understand this prioritizing at all," her mother said. "You can earn $5k a week building websites. That's $20k per month. One client a week at $5k. Go to work."

Monica was furious: "This is for your child to be on a huge network with a ginormous return. I am asking my mother for help with a television job and you're telling me to build websites and get to work? What? I am truly sick."

Her mom seemed unfazed by her tantrum and texted, *"Cover up your boobs and stop acting like an animal. You have young impressionable girls."*

Production for Season 4 was ramping up and Monica was the first one in line to volunteer. She had an existing relationship with casting, and with Jen and Sharrieff no longer around to prevent it, Monica was practically a shoo-in.

But she still appeared to be shocked and thrilled when she made the cut. It didn't seem possible! She was sitting where Jen had sat, and now she needed to act the part in order to keep the part. The pressure was overwhelming. She confessed to her friends that her finances were in dire straits, but that wasn't going to stop her from living the good life. The explanation was short and to the point: "Am I in foreclosure? Yes. Am I going to see Post Malone and Lizzo in concert back-to-back? Also yes. Fuck 'em."

She needed major funding to get camera ready, but money was

tight and tensions with her mom even tighter. She saved screenshots of all her fights with her mom and if she wasn't sharing them on Twitter, she shared them on all her group chats: *"I always pay you back! You're a FUCKKING trash bag mother. And I am done with YOU."*

Her mom would try to defend herself: "No, you don't always pay me! You promised to pay the car payment on time. You promised to pay the credit card in full within thirty days. There's still a balance. I'm done taking it up the ass."

Monica fought back: "Bipolar psycho. Mike literally got paid today! You lunatic!! You got $500 for the credit card and the car payment you fucking psycho bitch. Leave me the fuck alone!!! He just got paid today you asshole! How fucking dare you! You are a terrible parent and a disgusting excuse for a mother. Stay the fuck away from me and my children you mentally abusive and ill POS!"

Time was running out on her ability to prepare. Season 4 of *The Real Housewives of Salt Lake City* was ramping up to begin, and we had a kickoff meeting for the cast and crew. This was my first time meeting Monica. I sat through the entire meeting and never made the connection that I wasn't just meeting Monica Garcia, the newest Housewife to join the cast. I was also meeting Westleemae, the former frazzled assistant of Jen Shah; Monica Fowler, the Beauty Lab + Laser superfan; Monica Darnell, the "pick-me" witness in Jen Shah's federal case; MonicaNikiDalgado, the failed influencer with the misspelled name; and most importantly Reality Von Tease, the relentless internet troll fixated on *Housewives of SLC.*

A few days later, cameras were up, and filming officially began for season 4. In preparation, Monica was discussing strategy with anyone that would listen. "Just be yourself," was the advice she kept hearing, but that didn't help her. Being herself would reveal the person she had worked so hard at disguising. She wanted to be less like herself and more like Jen Shah. That's the formula she was counting on.

When the cast was leaked online, Monica's past began to emerge in random tweets and Instagram posts, accusing her of being a fraud. She put her Reality Von Tease persona back on and went on the attack posting daily under her anonymous burner accounts.

Someone Tweeted about her affair with her brother-in-law, another person threatened to expose that she couldn't make her car payments. Others claimed she was still married. Monica immediately defended herself and denied everything. She accused the trolls of lying and shamed them for attacking a struggling single mother: "You are disgussssssttttting."

As strong as her fight appeared on the outside, on the inside she was worried. Her friends convinced her that if she couldn't hide it she might as well lead with it. By getting ahead of the story, she could hopefully shut up the trolls that would inevitably come for her.

In one of our first scenes at a local consignment store, NameDroppers, Monica unabashedly proclaimed, "I fucked my brother-in-law for eighteen months!" It was shocking, it was brazen, and it accomplished exactly what she wanted.

Monica was clearly here to stay and here to play, so we welcomed her with open arms. This was our first season without Jen Shah so there was a lot at stake. We wanted the show to continue to be successful, but we also wanted the show to be different. Free from some of the dark toxicity and blatant deceit that had defined our years prior. We needed to come together as a cast and prove ourselves to each other all over again. Losing a Housewife is always a big deal, and we were still recovering from the loss of Jennie Ngyuen, Angie Harrington, and finally Jen Shah. It was clear that the network and production were putting everything they had into making Monica stick. And why wouldn't they? If only for lack of options? I felt the same things, and as a result, I became equally invested. The future of the show felt dependent on her fitting in.

Angie brought her to the "Fresh Powder, Fresh Start" season opener brunch in a ski suit she borrowed from her former best friend, to introduce her to the rest of the cast, and she jumped right into the fray, pelting snowballs and pithy compliments. No one asked her about her past associations with Jen, and Lisa said she didn't look anything like the same person she met in the airport years prior. She seemed to be a fun and feisty new addition to the group.

It wasn't until our first cast trip to Palm Springs that the cracks in her persona began to show, and they were as menacing and ominous as the cracks in her windshield.

Palm Springs was the setting for the Trixie Motel drag show, the espresso martinis at Copley's, the infamous security/waiter Chad, and Lisa's missing ring. It slipped off her hand in the outside airport bathroom and was never seen again. It was valued at over $60,000, and Monica accused Lisa of making too big a deal about losing it. She also turned on Angie, who had brought her on as her friend, and immediately took Meredith's side when they began feuding. She announced for the second time that she had "fucked her brother-in-law for eighteen months" and accused the other women of being boring and out of touch with middle America. She switched from crying about her finances to calling Lisa a "piece of shit" in Portuguese. It looked like a prepared line that she had been practicing in the mirror.

Monica continued to film throughout the season, and it became even more obvious that she was trying to be Jen, but she reverted to low-ball, immature arguments. She called Lisa ugly and she accused Angie's husband of sleeping with men, and the red flags really went up when she recounted a conversation with Lisa Barlow that never happened—well, at least that never happened with *her*. Lisa had discussed a private jet and a Snoop Dogg concert with Jen, but never with Monica. How would Monica know about Lisa's private conversations? She wondered aloud if Monica had access to Jen's security cameras. And she was exactly right. Monica had watched that conversation happen through the security cameras and confused it with something that had actually happened to her. Lisa confronted her immediately, confirming that there was no way Monica would know about that without illegally eavesdropping. It raised more than just alarm bells, it was totally creepy, but Lisa let it go. (And Lisa rarely lets things go!) We were halfway through the filming season and it didn't seem worth it.

Soon, it became clear that most of the drama from Monica was going to be about her mother, Linda, and their dysfunctional relationship. Their scenes were filled with drama, but the real theater occurred online through their leaked text messages, videos, and aggressive Tweeting wars. At Angie's Greek Easter event, Monica and her mother got into a public row, with Monica alleging she fell down the stairs (video at the reunion refuted this claim), and Linda went home alone in a "shitbox" Uber (type of shitbox unknown).

Then, when the episode aired, Monica threatened to sue Angie for not having a hand railing on her staircase and she secretly recorded a video of her and her mother fighting about her airtime on the show: *"You're an actress! This is a reality show that you worked hard to get on and you failed. The only thing you did was unite those four assholes."* And she was right. We were united. The way she acted was strangely familiar to all of us.

But she was on the cast, and we were forced to play along.

SCREENSHOTS!

In the weeks leading up to our trip to Bermuda, Monica's life appeared to be falling apart, and her personalities appeared to be changing dramatically from one minute to the next.

First, she emotionally shut down when we announced the trip to Bermuda even though the whole thing was centered around visiting *her* family for *her* birthday. And she started to backtrack on a lot of the things she had shared with the group: she wasn't actually divorced, just separated, and they still texted every day, exchanging sexy selfies and sweet encouragements; she claimed she had "grown up going to Bermuda," but only shared memories from one visit when she was practically a toddler.

Then, the situation for me became personal and more complicated. I discovered that Monica had several customer profiles at Beauty Lab + Laser. I realized that she had come to Beauty Lab at different times using different names, and on one of those visits using one of those identities, she had charged thousands of dollars in services and skipped out on the bill. I was totally shocked. How could she have come on the show knowing this would be discovered? Beauty Lab is a very customer-oriented company. We know our clients and we care about them. We don't have grifters that steal from us.

I wanted to expose her immediately, but I felt protective of the information, and I wasn't sure if it was HIPAA protected. When you run a med spa, customer data is protected by law, even if they have stolen from you. There was also a small part of me that felt bad for Monica. I knew that she was struggling financially and the stories she had told me about her life had definitely tugged on my heartstrings. I had paid for all of our clothing purchases at NameDroppers, and had splurged on a Loewe bag for her birthday. I didn't want to kick her while she was down. Maybe there was a logical explanation? But what she had done felt sneaky—it felt dirty and it felt wrong. It also felt incredibly brazen. Like someone else I knew. Who else dares to go on a reality TV show when they have insurmountable skeletons in their closet? I'll give you one guess, and she's currently serving a sentence in Bryan Federal Prison Camp.

I wanted to call her out and tell everyone I knew, including the network, but I said nothing because more than anything, I wanted her to work out as a castmate and I wanted her to end up being a great addition to our show. It was the same reason I had stayed quiet about Jen when I knew she was lying.

I wasn't sure what to do—in terms of *Housewives* or Beauty Lab + Laser. I was pretty sure I would confront her at some point but I didn't know how or when. I decided to just play it by ear and see how things went on our trip.

Monica didn't give me much to work with in Bermuda. Her personality was all over the place. She attacked me for not wanting to talk about my twenty-year-old daughter's sex life and was angrier and more aggressive than ever. She acted defeated and defensive and began backtracking on all of her stories about her family, her home life, and her history. This was supposed to be her celebratory birthday trip, but she was either on her phone, brooding silently, or picking fights for no reason. Then, when walking on the beach, she confessed to me that she'd be the type of person to create a fake account and send fake DMs in order to spread dirt about someone. It was creepy. But it was another thing I consciously overlooked, just like everybody else. We were rooting for Monica and focusing on her strengths, not on the holes in her story or the ways she didn't fit in.

Meanwhile, off camera, the team that had launched Reality Von Tease was falling apart. Monica was on the outs with all but one of the remaining members, and her paranoia about being discovered grew stronger every day. In the weeks leading up to our trip, Tenesha, my hairstylist, and Monica had a major falling out, and it rattled Monica. Now that we were leaving for Bermuda, it seemed like the secret was about to implode. Tenesha confessed to my makeup artist, Jill, the secret she was keeping about Monica and asked her what she should do. "Tell Heather immediately," Jill said.

When she finally called me there wasn't a lot of small talk: "There's something you need to know about Monica," she said calmly. "Monica is Reality Von Tease."

It was that simple of a sentence. That's all she had to say. My stomach dropped, and everything came into play. Suddenly, the money she owed Beauty Lab was the last of my concerns.

I knew the name immediately. I remembered distinctly when it had launched on Instagram and when it had gone viral with the leaked security footage. We had fought about the page as a cast in season 2. In our confessionals, we quoted things we heard Jen say in the leaked audios: *"How many people do you need to make one fucking dress?" "Did your parents teach you how to lie?"* And now we were filming with the woman who had recorded her.

It didn't seem possible. There are background checks and vetting and thorough research done before you can be cast as a Housewife. How had she slipped through undetected? But the more I thought about it the more it all made sense. Finally, I understood how and why Monica knew so much about all of our lives. The mask was off and her gig was up. Reality Von Tease had been someone deep on the inside of Jen's team. And now that person was deep on the inside of my friend group, my cast, and the television show that had changed my life.

But I had to be sure. If I was going to confront her, I needed to be positive my case was bulletproof. So, I cross-checked my sources and reached out to another friend who worked at Meta. It's pretty easy to track down the original owner of a troll account when that owner has bragged about it publicly and has continued running a network of burner accounts. But I needed receipts and I didn't have any. It was bigger than her just running Reality Von Tease, it was her catfishing all of us, the cast, the crew, the network, and the viewing audience.

I had been in a situation like this before, and I knew Monica was going to deny everything. If she had made it this far under false pretenses, why would anyone think she would cave now? I needed actual proof, but I wasn't even sure what I was looking for. I was still reeling from learning of Tenesha's involvement, but she was willing to put herself on the line in order to set the record straight. She had a full crisis of conscience and unburdened herself from the secret with a full confession. It was brave and it was bold, and I will forever be grateful that she came forward and told the truth. I asked her to send me any evidence she had.

The mansion we were staying at in Bermuda was remarkable for a lot of things, but not its WiFi connectivity. As I was getting ready for dinner, my mind was thudding with this new information. I needed to see the evidence from every source. They said they'd sent it, but it wasn't coming through. I paced around my room while the iCloud kept a persistent downloading-status circle flickering on the screen. It seemed to take hours for the information to appear on my phone, and as each screenshot slowly downloaded one by one, I began to become more enraged. I called everyone I could think of to help me sort it out: "Hey. What did you find out? Are you fucking kidding me? I can't believe it's her. I'm freaking the fuck out."

I was at a loss, standing alone at a fork in the road. I was exhausted, and this felt like more than I had signed up for. What would this mean for our friendships? What would it mean for the show? I didn't want to stage a coup, all I wanted to do was go home.

I felt deeply betrayed. I had been a friend to Monica. I had cried with her, I had championed her, and I had worked hard to make her feel included in the cast. I thought I was her friend. Clearly, I had been fooled.

There were only a few hours left before dinner, and I was processing the magnitude of the situation while figuring out what I was going to do. I debated whether or not I should even tell production. There is a cat-and-mouse game always at play when you are working with producers because the untold stories and the secrets we are trying to hide often make the best television. The producer's job is not to protect our reputations or feelings; it is to produce a good show. It's great when everything is aligned, but sometimes our motivations are in direct conflict. Maybe they had cast Monica specifically because she *was* a troll blogger. Maybe casting knew, but production didn't; maybe production knew, but Bravo didn't. Maybe everyone knew, and I was the last one invited to the big Reality Von Tease reveal. But something in my gut told me this wasn't true. The secret was too big, it was too devastating, and it could undermine the honesty and vulnerability of the franchise. They would never have hired her if they had known her secret.

Our showrunner, Lori Gordon, knew that something was up, and came into my room cautiously. She sat with me as everything just poured out from its beginning to its very bitter end. She didn't really understand what any of it meant or how what Monica had done was any different from your average Housewife trolling. But this *was* different, and I told her that she might not understand why it was important, but that Meredith, Lisa, and Whitney would. They were the only ones who would know exactly what I was talking about and why it was such a big deal. I wanted them to be the first ones I told. She agreed and asked where I'd like to tell them.

"Somewhere private," I replied.

Private to production meant the beach right in front of our mansion, with a flying drone, full audio, and a team of cameramen stationed at a respectable distance.

As I stood there alone on the beach, I was scared. I didn't want to cause problems—not for production, not even for Monica. Questions swirled in my head as my stomach tossed and flipped in fear. I had done it again: I had befriended and believed in someone who was not who they pretended to be. And who had no intention of being my friend. I had been in that situation before with Jen, and it did not end well. I did not want to go down that road again. Would I swallow this information? Or would I honor how I felt at that moment, spit it out, and say, "not today and never again will I fall for this two-bit bullshit"?

I stood out there on that beach waiting for everyone to come down and meet me. Production sent them down one by one. We had never discussed Reality Von Tease amongst ourselves, but I was banking on the fact that they would know exactly who I was talking about and that they would have the same reaction I did.

When Lisa approached, she started crying before I even spoke. Everyone could feel the tension. "Monica is not who she says she is," I said through muffled tears, as the wind whipped around us. "She's not our friend. She's someone that has schemed and worked to infiltrate our friend group. And the name that you all know her as—the woman whose birthday we celebrated; who we have been trying to champion, support, and defend is . . . Reality Von Tease. Pull it up on your phone. Released all the videos about Jen? That was Monica that recorded them. All of those audio recordings and behind the scenes secrets that have hurt and affected our lives [and] that we have fought over for three years were all posted, curated, and spread by her. I want to confront her at dinner tonight, and I want you guys to back me up."

As they each reacted to what I said, our relationships transformed. We went from being friends and castmates to being allies and sisters.

We were not just four women on a beach, we were *all* women on *all* beaches. We were a sisterhood. We stood there huddled like the Avengers and talked for over an hour. It was a meeting of the minds and no one held back. We put all of our dirt and suspicions about Monica out there into the universe. Meredith revealed that she believed Monica had been in disguise on her security footage when a clutch went missing. Lisa remembered rumblings about Jen's former assistant conducting drive-bys in front of our homes and watching Jen's security footage. Whitney mentioned hearing about her skipping out on bills all over town, including a hair extension salon where it ran into the thousands. There was so much to discuss that I didn't even need to mention that she had never paid for her services from Beauty Lab.

When we put all our cards on the table collectively, we realized that every single one of us had shelved our doubts and questions in order to be a friend to Monica. And that was something we had also done with Jen. But we quickly learned to ignore the red flags, the alarm bells, and the fact that things just didn't add up.

Everything that Monica threatened made us realize everything we appreciated about each other. We knew each other's families, lives, businesses, and backgrounds. We knew that, despite all our pretenses and facades, who we were beneath it all wasn't make believe. We hadn't invented a character out of thin air just to get cast on a television show.

As friends and as enemies, we had more in common with each other than we would ever have with someone trying to con us like Monica. It didn't matter which identity she led with—Westleemae, or Ms. Fowler, or MonicaNikiDalgado—none of them were authentic. None of it mattered. When you let a clown into the castle, the clown doesn't become a king; the castle becomes a circus.

In that moment we bonded—we all loved the show we were on,

the sanctity of the Housewives franchise, and the authenticity that we each dared to show up with. On that beach, we all looked at each other and then they looked at me and without questioning said, "We have your back!"

Once I knew that I was going to confront her at dinner, not a minute went by that I wasn't rehearsing what I would say. My only fear was that I would not have the courage to do it—that I wouldn't have the right words, that I wouldn't be able to say it all the "right way," and that she wouldn't admit to her scheme. But I reassured myself by restating the fact that this was proven and that this was confirmed. In fact, I had her proven formula: *"Receipts! Proof! Timeline! Screenshots!"* I didn't need to doubt; I just needed to put a stop to it.

I loved being a Housewife, I loved our city, I loved our show, and I loved these women. I had put my heart and soul into being Monica's friend and she had shit all over them. It felt familiar. I wasn't going to repeat the pattern. As we went around the table at dinner, we challenged each other to share an unsolved mystery about each other in honor of the Bermuda Triangle. Everyone at the table (besides Angie and Monica) knew that despite the issues we needed to resolve with each other, the big confrontation of the night was going to be Reality Von Tease. But we were on our own. Production was not prompting us, there was no real direction to the conversation, and there was a huge risk that our plan would fail.

I was so nervous, I kept squeezing Angie's hand under the table. She was confused at why I was so worked up, but she didn't question it, and instead kept refilling my water glass and reassuring me that everything was going to be okay.

When it was my turn to speak, I turned to Monica and said, "You are not someone who wants to be our friend. You are someone that has profited off our pain and exploited our good nature. I know who you really are, who you really are is the cyberbully, internet troll, Reality Von Tease."

She denied it at first—"That's not true, entirely..."—but no one believed a word she said. Meredith confronted her about the security footage. Whitney confronted her about the things she had said online. Lisa confronted her about her constant drive-bys and pathetic obsessions. Angie confronted her about all the lies she had spread about her family. She denied everything, over and over, calling us crazy, saying we were wrong, pretending to be innocent. But we were right and it was all true.

By the end of the night it was clear she had run out of excuses and had nothing to say that could explain her behavior. She got up from the table and began to walk away. "Leave my shoes," Meredith admonished, and Monica kicked off the sandals she had been borrowing and walked barefoot down the hill back into the house.

We did not have to talk to Monica again until the season 4 reunion taped in New York City almost six months later. That night, after we confronted her, she walked away from the table and took her microphone off. We stayed outside, crying and talking and replaying everything that had just happened. Once security told us that she was gone, we went inside and sat around a table in the kitchen. The crew told us that they'd taken her to a hotel near the airport, and that she was booked on a separate flight home to Utah. There was no way she was ever coming back, and we breathed a sigh of relief hoping we'd never have to see her again. It was a very tumultuous night, and we all felt the power of it.

When we got home, we slowly realized that, despite the bombshell that exploded in Bermuda, there were still confessionals that needed to be filmed and a television show to be made. *We were still in bed with this bitch.* It became clear that she was going to be in our peripheral vision everywhere we went until the truth about her was revealed. And we understood the risks we had taken on by exposing her. A new Housewife isn't exactly expendable, and networks don't make casting decisions based on hurt feelings or troll accounts. We were risking our own positions in the cast, but we were determined to stick together.

We weren't going to play to ratings or play to the audience or even play to the network. We were going to play to what was authentic to us as a group of friends. And there was nothing authentic about Monica Darnell-Fowler-Dalgado-Garcia. No one wanted this imposter troll anywhere near us, our families, our businesses, or our lives.

The production company and Warner Bros. launched an immediate investigation, interviewing everyone involved and reviewing a stockpile of receipts, proof, timelines, and screenshots, filling in all the details of how Monica "the Housewife" ever came to be. When the dust settled, we felt vindicated. Monica was on an island, isolated from the rest of us, and there was no future for her in our friend group or on the show. When season 5 began filming, she was not invited back, and we all breathed a sigh of relief.

At the end of the day, there's a lot you can fake—your identity, your name, your background, your true motivations. But the one thing you can't fake is friendship. And at its core, that's what we wanted our show to really be about. The Monicon truly brought us together as a cast in the most unifying way possible. Regardless of where we were at before, that day on the beach, the Salt Lake snowflakes started a storm that would change the way we counted on each other forever. And I hope it lasts: *I don't want the world, but I'll take this city.*

OUTRO/EPILOGUE

When I was a nineteen-year-old girl on my mission in the South of France, I wrote a letter to my best friend wherein I expressed that I didn't want to be "very happy." I didn't want to live a life of compulsory obligation to a man, to the church, or to anybody but myself. I wanted to live an extraordinary life, but I can't be sure I ever really thought that life would come to pass.

I'll never be Kate Winslet, Toni Morrison, Ann Landers, or Barbara Walters, but the life I'm living now is bigger than anything my teenage heart could've imagined. I didn't change the world for the greater good, but I changed the world for myself, for my family, and for the generations that will follow. I feel like I blazed a new trail in a direction I didn't know was possible, and if the only ones it benefits are my daughters, then that is good enough for me.

They say that well-behaved women never make history, and now I finally understand that striving to always be good required self-betrayal that kept me from being *ME*. When I look at younger pictures of myself and reflect on the collected stories of my life—just a few of which I've shared in this book—I recognize the struggle I felt as a child, as a teenager, as a young wife, and as a new mother, to be and become GOOD above everything and to ignore the Good-Time Girl that has always been inside of me. I was ashamed of her and afraid of her, but now, it is only by honoring her that I can feel the joy and fulfillment of embracing the person I was born to be. I'm forever grateful for the fans and the friends that I've met throughout my life, and I'm humbled that they've rallied around me as I learned to live as my most authentic self.

I've come a long way from being that little girl filling out baseball scorecards in San Bernardino with a cheek full of Big League Chew. From the Wee Wetter Alarm through to stolen kisses in Tijuana, from sober dorm parties at BYU through to premiere parties at Sundance, I've changed in extraordinary ways. But, at the end of the day, through it all, my core has remained the same.

And so, it is with full confidence and pride that I suggest we raise a glass of your choosing—a glass of milk, a Diet Coke, a Vida Tequila—to that unshifting, unwavering, uncompromising core deep down in the root of each of us. Because, as it turns out, being a Good-Time Girl isn't about baring your tits; it's about baring your heart.

ACKNOWLEDGMENTS

There are so many people I want to acknowledge . . . but who even reads the Acknowledgments anyway.

I'll start by first thanking my parents, for giving me an amazing childhood with enough core memories to write two books—and if I'm lucky perhaps someday even a third. Thank you to my siblings for motivating me to keep on succeeding. The sky is the limit!

A huge thank you to my friend and handsome book agent, Steve Troha. One day I'll write something that you'll actually want to read, and I look forward to that day. I also look forward to the cookbook you promised me. To my brilliant and insightful editor, Natasha Simons— you make me a better writer every time I take your advice. To my amazing and talented writing partner, John Jardin—you've advanced from being the frog in my pocket to being my favorite friend for "coffee talk." That may sound demeaning, but it's truly the highest compliment I could ever give.

To my entire team at Gallery—I love you! I love you! I love you!

And I don't care who knows it! Thank you to Jen Bergstrom for making me feel like a real writer, not just a *Real Housewife*. Thank you to Mia Robertson for laughing at my jokes and making me feel seen and understood. Thank you to Lauren Carr, my fearless publicist, for teaching me that I can filter my thoughts in interviews and that I don't have to tell everyone everything all the time.

To the women of *The Real Housewives of Salt Lake City*, thank you for the fun and the fights and the frivolity. This show truly rescued me in so many ways. And as such, you are all my benefactors. To Shed Media, Lori Gordon, Tamara Blaich, Casey Allan, and the incredible production team. Thank you for putting up with my neuroses and always editing me in THE BEST POSSIBLE WAY. To the incredible executives at Bravo and NBCUniversal, including Zaddy Andy *("Hi bebe!")*—you've made all my dreams come true.

To the business that pulled me out from the deep—Beauty Lab + Laser. Dre, you make me want to be a better man. You're the yin to my yang, and I couldn't do any of this without you. Dreather forever!

To my children—I love you. I love our life. I'm happiest when we're together. I never dreamed things could be this good. And now, my only dream is to keep it going forever.

To all of the Bad Mormons and Good-Time Girls of the world—I am eternally grateful for the community we've built together over the last few years. You inspire me every day and have redefined what it means to be "good." May you continue to let your truest self shine bright! Keep on dancing!!

And lastly—perhaps most importantly—to all the other Huldah's out there floating around . . . don't hang your head in shame! Let yourself be known: *"Mom! Mom! There's a Huldah!"*